IN MEMORY OF:

Mrs. Doris Ayres

PRESENTED BY:

Mr. & Mrs. Michael Roseberry

Frank O. Gehry

Selected Works: 1969 to Today

A FIREFLY BOOK

Published by Firefly Books Ltd. 2007

First printing

Publisher Cataloging-in-Publication Data (U.S.)

Mathewson, Casey, C. M.
     Frank O. Gehry : selected works : 1969 to today / Casey C. M. Mathewson.
[608] p. : ill., photos. ; cm.
Includes bibliographical references and index.
Summary: A selective retrospective of Frank O. Gehry's most important designs. Includes essays detailing his use of technology and diverse materials, and of light, form and sculpture.
ISBN-13: 978-1-55407-276-7
ISBN-10: 1-55407-276-X
1. Gehry, Frank O., 1929– . II. Title.
720.92 dc22   NA737.G44.M384 2007

Library and Archives Canada Cataloguing in Publication

Mathewson, Casey C. M
     Frank O. Gehry : selected works : 1969 to today / Casey C.M. Mathewson.
Previously published in German and English.
ISBN-13: 978-1-55407-276-7
ISBN-10: 1-55407-276-X
     1. Gehry, Frank O., 1929–. I. Gehry, Frank O., 1929– II. Title.
NA737.G44A4 2007   720.92   C2007-903756-9

Published in the United States by
Firefly Books (U.S.) Inc
P.O. Box 1338, Ellicott Station
Buffalo, New York 14205

Published in Canada by
Firefly Books Ltd.
66 Leek Crescent
Richmond Hill, Ontario L4B 1H1

Editor, author, layout, and typesetting mab - Casey C.M. Mathewson, Berlin www.ma-b.net
Plan diagrams mab - Anna Borgman
Production artwork-factory.com
Picture editing Fabio Ricci
Idea and concept Peter Feierabend, Casey C.M. Mathewson

Cover design Hufton+Crow/VIEW/artur

Printed in China

Casey C.M. Mathewson

Frank O. Gehry
Selected Works: 1969 to Today

FIREFLY BOOKS

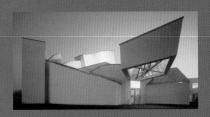

Form, Function, Sculpture

Art or architecture?
Gehry's work dissolves the
conventional borders between
the two disciplines.

Form, Function, Sculpture

In the 1960s, when Frank Gehry decided to leave the rigidity of then dominant late modernism behind, nobody, least of all the architect himself, could know where the path would lead.

Rather than accepting the drab conventionality of the architectural marketplace, Gehry seeks creative dialogue with artists. The work of people like painter Mark Rothko, whose paintings are abstract yet deeply spiritual, convinced him that architecture can do more than fulfill mere pragmatic functions.

He uses the artist's devices, especially the sculptor's, to imbue his buildings with a holistic depth that never derails into rigidity. His is an architecture that elevates the chaos, fast-lane superficiality and eternal sunshine of his hometown, Los Angeles, to poetry.

With the demise of postmodernism in the early 1990s, Gehry offered an alternative. By rejuvenating the guiding paradigms of modernism, he shows that the long-dead believed principle "form follows function" can be interpreted in a myriad of new ways. Additionally, Gehry skillfully uses new technologies to realize expressionistic forms that allow the visionary utopian visions of early modernism to become reality.

Armed with ebullient yet uncompromising creativity, Gehry continues his ceaseless search for new solutions. As such, this book documents the inquisitive exploration of an architect for whom "architecture is an obsession."

Vitra Design Museum, Weil am Rhein, Germany, 1987–89

Gehry's seemingly free forms, such as these of the Neue Zollhof project in Düsseldorf's revamped port district, are all but coincidental.

New information-age technology
now allows creation of even
the most complex geometric
composition.

Guggenheim Museum, Bilbao, Spain, 1991–97

Gehry's work in Los Angeles has long translated the stage
and set–like artificiality of the media capital into built form.
The Disney Concert Hall (1988–2003) is the most prominent
commission yet built in his hometown.

Beginnings in Los Angeles:
Hymn to Artificiality

In the 1980s, an era in which many architects were preoccupied with neoclassical postmodernism, Frank Gehry suddenly surfaced on the international architectural stage. His buildings draw inspiration from the artificiality of Los Angeles.

They are imbued with a sense of inclusiveness and a serious yet laid-back approach to site, program and form. By consequently pursuing an architecture firmly rooted in art, Gehry offered an exciting alternative to the superficial historicism prevailing at the time.

Whereas the 1980s projects of his Los Angeleno contemporaries, such as Charles Moore, seem wistful, almost comical, Gehry's works strive to achieve a profound synthesis of architecture and art. This is an architect who rejects the orthogonal monotony of late modernism. At the same time he is engaged in a serious search for a new architecture far removed from historical allusions. The key to the poetic nature of the early work lie in Gehry's uncanny ability to translate the superficiality of Los Angeles into an architecture that transcends and stands above it as a poetic hymn to artificiality.

Claes Oldenburg and Coosje van Bruggen,
Chiat/Day Building, Los Angeles, 1991

Claes Oldenburg, Tool Gate
Vitra Design Museum, Weil/Rhein, 1989

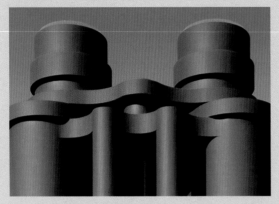

In times in which appearance is often deemed more important than content, many buildings seem composed of scarcely more than interchangeable skin. Gehry reverses this tendency by allowing the inner life of his buildings to generate their outer form. Revealed structural elements — tilting wood beams, exposed sheet rock, corrugated sheet metal and chain link — form the palette of materials for the early works. These are often composed as collage-like scenarios constructed in everyday "cheapskate" materials, an approach to architecture Gehry developed in collaboration with artists with whom he maintains long-standing friendships. By the mid-1960s Gehry increasingly distanced himself from an architectural establishment bounded by the dogmatic confines of "form follows function" ideology. He found inspiration in lively dialogue with artists who commissioned him with small projects. The Danziger House and Studio in Hollywood (1964–65) and the Davis Studio and Residence in Malibu offered creative freedom to experiment with new forms far removed from the constraints of formalism.

During his studies at the University of Southern California (1949–54) the young architect, born in Toronto in 1929, went by his given name, Frank Owen Goldberg. At completion of studies in 1954 he changed his name to Gehry. In the first years working in the profession at Victor Gruen Associates in Los Angeles (1953–55/1957–61) he completed his training in the

Above: Artworks underscore the respective
architectural intention of each project.

Frank O. Gehry, A Rose for Lilly
Disney Concert Hall, Los Angeles, 2003

Anish Kapoor, Cloud Gate
Millennium Park, Chicago, 2004

then common vein with minute perfection in design as the highest priority. But the proving ground of his first large commission, the Steeves House (1958–59), convinced him that this perfection in design and craftsmanship could not be attained in the economic reality of 1950s Los Angeles. "My artist friends, people like Jasper Johns, Bob Rauschenberg, Ed Kienholz and Claes Oldenburg, were working with very inexpensive materials — broken wood and paper — and they were making beauty. These were not superficial details. They were direct. It raised the question of what was beautiful. I chose to use the craft available, and to work with the craftsmen and make a virtue out of their limitations."

Gehry's architecture increasingly focuses on the definition of enigmatic forms founded in the art of sculpture. At the same time, the work transcends the limitations of art and successfully addresses the pragmatic nature of architecture as the art form that must also meet practical needs. The intense dialogue with artists leads to ever more refined sculptural compositions that achieve architectural significance without becoming rigid or monumental.

In 1984, while commenting on the 1964 Danziger House, he said he "was also interested in the idea of connection, of putting pieces together, in a way very similar to what I am still doing. I guess we only have one idea in our lives."

At the construction site of the Vitra Design Museum in Weil am Rhein, Germany.

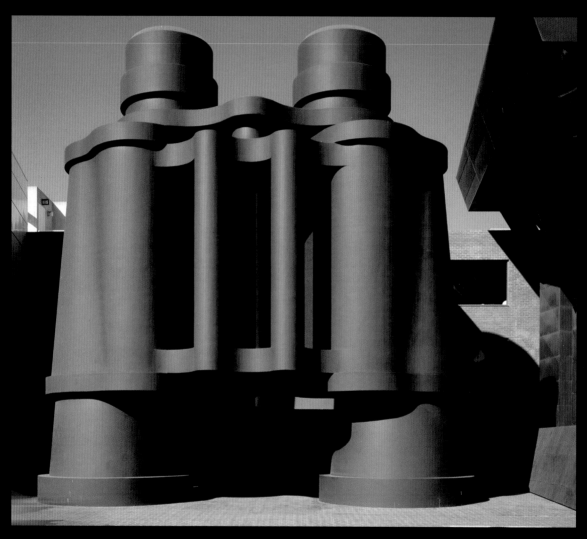

Above: The Chiat Building's (1985–91) entrance is marked with a sculpture by Claes Oldenburg and Coosje van Bruggen. Right: The whimsical nature of the early works gave way to a more serious Gehry from the large commissions of the 1990s on, but the light, relaxed quality in his work remained, as evidenced here in the suspended ceiling of the Disney Concert Hall (1988–2003).

Over the years Gehry has continuously refined and perfected his understanding of his buildings as sculptural compositions that can elevate his architecture to fulfill more than mere functional requirements.
Above: Edgemar Project, Los Angeles, 1984–88

Californian breakthrough
on the Venice Beach
beachwalk, the Norton
House (1982–84).

From Outsider to Rising Star:
Improvisation and Composition

During the 1970s Gehry increasingly distanced himself from the rigidity of late modernism. His answer? "Cheapskate architecture" composed as a collage made up of "junk" materials. His best field of experimentation in this period is offered by his own house in Santa Monica (1977–78; 1991–94). Here, free from convention and expectation, he developed a design approach that forged the path for the future projects. Upon first sight, the collage of unpainted plywood, chain link, corrugated metal and exposed wood framing seems coincidental, almost destructive. But upon further study one discovers that nothing has been left to chance here. Unsightly connections, abrupt transitions between materials, a kitchen floor in asphalt — all of these are consciously chosen statements that translate Gehry's personal answer to Los Angeles' chaotic culture into architecture.

Soon met with accolades and prizes, his own house served as the point of departure for further residential designs. With his plans for the Norton House (1982–84), the Wosk House (1981–84) and the Winton House (1982–87) he honed his architectural ideas to perfection. Here the individual building volumes are increasingly differentiated into expressive pieces that are skillfully composed to form a sculptural still life.

Edgemar Project, Santa Monica, 1984 –88

In addition to the private residences, Gehry designed ever-larger public buildings
that made him the rising star among the cities' architects. From 1970-82 he executed
renovation and conversion work to transform the legendary Hollywood Bowl amphitheater
into a premier venue for the Los Angeles Philharmonic Orchestra. In 1980 he realized an
acoustic scheme here by incorporating seemingly floating sound-deflecting spheres into
the famous arched proscenium. It was this project that increased his notoriety, especially
for potential public and commercial clients.

The Santa Monica Place Shopping Center (1972–80), his largest project of the 1970s,
allowed Gehry to apply new ideas to a large-scale commercial project. The entrance front
steps back from the street to create a well-proportioned entrance plaza. Oblique building
elements are used as open terraces and pavilions to reduce the optical massiveness of the
building and incorporate human scale. A light-filled, roofed passage continues the public
street-space into the building. The southern side of the parking structure conjures up
unforgettable imagery. Gehry hangs blue chain link four stories high across the entire
300 foot long structure. Huge letters of silver chain link are affixed here to create a giant,
half-transparent sign.

Above: Gehry's use of everyday "junk" materials to
create poetic forms was perfected in the 1970s and 80s.

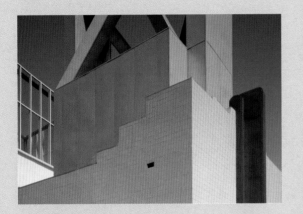

The projects for the Loyola Law School (1978–98), the California Aerospace Museum (1982–84), the Goldwyn Library in Hollywood (1982–86), the Edgemar Project (1984–88) and Institute Buildings for UCLA Irvine (1983–88) all see Gehry perfecting his repertoire of collage-like building complexes, achieving an ever-gaining poetic quality. The increasing size of the projects allowed Gehry to envision village-like complexes that created especially interesting urban spaces. At the same time he refined the materials used like an improvising jazz musician searching for the nuance of the "just right" tone. The construction details became more refined and solid, but the overall impression of the buildings remains improvised and simultaneously composed.

The mid-1980s see Gehry attaining US-wide success. The Yale Psychiatric Institute (1985–89), the Iowa Laser Laboratory (1987–92), the Visual Arts Center in Toledo (1989–94) and the Weisman Museum in Minneapolis (1990–93) formed a series of creative buildings for culture and university use where he successfully translated his Los Angeles-based architectural language to accommodate other climates and regional traditions.

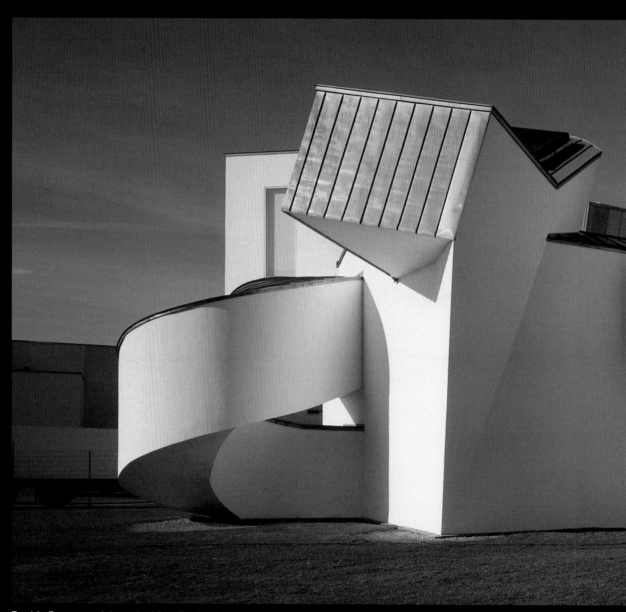

For his European debut, the Vitra Design Museum in Weil am Rhein Germany (1987–89),
Gehry designed a moving sculptural composition.

ne 1980s saw Gehry refining his vocabulary to create an architecture of typically Californian easiness.

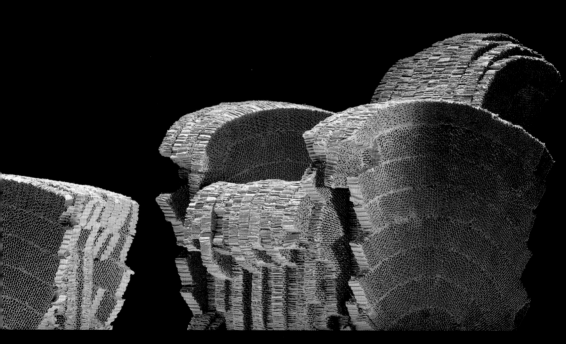

For the Easy Edges and Experimental Edges furniture lines Gehry experiments with ordinary cardboard.

Above: Edges Easy Chair, 1979–82
Right: Easy Edges, 1969–73

Gehry promoting his
Bentwood furniture series
manufactured by Knoll
International.

The "Bilbao Effect":
The Trajectory to Global Architect

Meanwhile, recognized not only as an architect with extensive building experience but also as an eminent architectural scholar, Gehry taught at the best architectural schools in the United States. Rice University, Cooper Union, Harvard, Yale, UCLA and MIT offered him the possibility to develop his thoughts on an academic platform together with gifted students. In 1988 his work opened the epochal "Deconstructivist Architecture" exhibition at the New York Museum of Modern Art. From this point forward Gehry was at the center of a group of architects — Coop, Himmelblau, Eisenman, Hadid, Koolhaas, Libeskind and Tschumi — who would work worldwide on the prestigious commissions of the 1990s.

The year 1989, which marked the fall of the Iron Curtain and hailed a new start for oppressed societies across Eastern Europe, also brought a milestone in Frank Gehry's career. The architect won both the competition for Los Angeles' new Philharmonic Hall, the Walt Disney Concert Hall, and was awarded the Pritzker Prize, architecture's most coveted award.

Gehry's Japanese premiere, the Fishdance Restaurant in Kobe, marked his explosive breakthrough onto the international scene in 1987. His first building in Europe, the Vitra Design Museum (1987–89), followed soon

Guggenheim Museum, Bilbao, 1991–97

Nationale Nederlanden Building, Prague, 1992–96

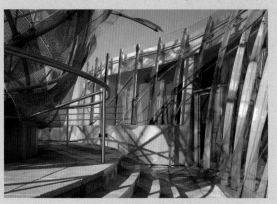

thereafter. The direction for the important buildings of the 1990s, often built outside the United States, became clear. Regions that profited from the democratic transformation in Europe — Barcelona, Prague and Berlin — provided the stage for some of Gehry's most creative work. Cities worldwide increasingly discovered the potential of "landmark" architecture to redefine their images. Gehry set the standard for this phenomenon with his Guggenheim Museum in Bilbao, Spain (1994–97).

The Disney Concert Hall in Los Angeles — completed in 2003 after execution of 30,000 drawings and 16 years of planning and building — culminated this phase with a truly exceptional building. As the major work in his hometown, it is especially convincing due to its acceptance by the demanding musicians and concertgoers who deem its acoustics as nearly perfect. This approval served as a confirmation of Gehry's design process, in which the concert hall space is developed with dozens of models and the rest of the building is then organized to huddle around this grand space.

Even though his projects continuously increase in size Gehry takes the time to design buildings for charitable organizations. For the Ronald McDonald House and Maggie's Cancer Centre the architect charged no fees for his services. In both Gehry created cheerful yet dignified places of caring where architecture plays a special part in healing.

Above: Gehry's major commissions in the 1990s were increasingly located abroad.

Pariser Platz 3, Berlin, 1994–99

Der Neue Zollhof, Düsseldorf, 1994–2001

In 1989, in his Pritzker acceptance speech, Gehry described his vision of architecture's unique role within the arts:

> I am obsessed with architecture. It is true. I am restless, trying to find myself as an architect, and how best to contribute in this world filled with contradiction, disparity, and inequality, even passion and opportunity. It is a world in which our values and priorities are constantly being challenged. It is simplistic to expect a single right answer. Architecture is a small piece of this human equation, but for those of us who practice it, we believe in its potential to make a difference, to enlighten and to enrich the human experience, to penetrate the barriers of misunderstanding and provide a beautiful context for life's drama.

A noncompromising dedication to architecture as art, combined with the laid-back Californian way of life, characterizes all of Gehry's work. As an obsessive perfectionist he is engaged in a demanding investigation of ways to unite expressive form and utilitarian function. And today his search for the essence of architecture as an expression of the paradoxes of our time continues with the same dedication and ceaseless conviction. The result? Buildings that prove "better is possible."

Disney Concert Hall, Los Angeles, 1988–2003

Achieving urban renewal through "signature" buildings is a trend that Gehry instigated in the 1990s with buildings such as the Neuer Zollhof complex on the banks of the Rhine river in Düsseldorf, Germany (1994–2001, above) and the Vila Olimpica on Barcelona's Mediterranean beachfront built just prior to the 1992 Olympic Games in Barcelona, Spain (1991, right).

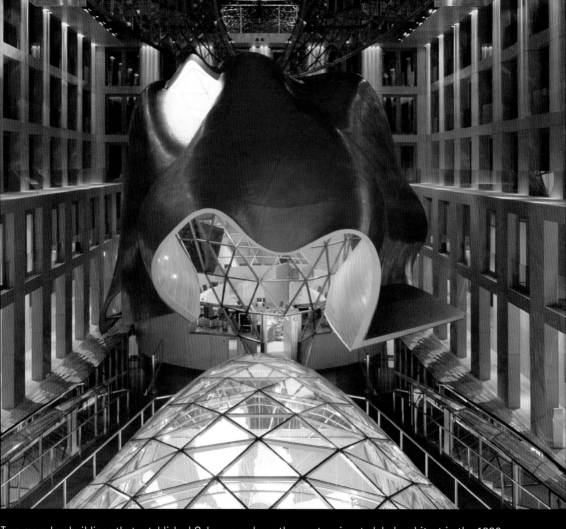

Two more key buildings that established Gehry as perhaps the most eminent global architect in the 1990s.
Above: Pariser Platz 3 in Berlin, Germany (1994–99)
Right: Guggenheim Museum in Bilbao, Spain (1991–97)

Millennium Park Chicago 2004: an architectural sculpture as the final result of countless sketches and models.

Metamorphosis of Idea to Form: Gehry's Design Process

To facilitate his inquisitive search for the optimal form Gehry uses a probing design process that he developed from the outset of his career. Since 1990 architectural software has also played an extensive role in designing complex forms, which can hence be built within the tight budget constraints increasingly present on every project.

Just as an artist develops a painting layer on layer, Gehry uses a combination of creative tools to envision his final design. Loose-hand sketches are used to define the central design idea of each project. Massing models, which distribute the building's program on the site, form the next step of the design process. Site models in varied scales are used to confirm the knowledge gained through the first hand-sketches and rough massing models. Gehry believes it is especially important to contrast different scale models against other. The resultant jump in scale forces him to remain flexible and not decide on any one idea too quickly.

In addition to preparing architectural design models in the think tank of his office, Gehry spends as much time as possible with the clients and users of the future buildings. As soon as the program is favorably distributed in the

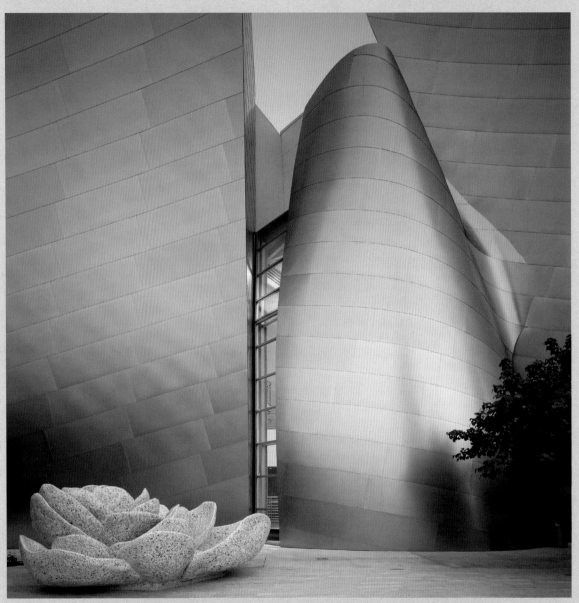

Disney Concert Hall, Los Angeles, USA, 1988–2003

various model scales and the client's confirmation is attained, he goes into another stage of hand sketching. These more detailed sketches form the basis for comprehensive architectural models, which are formed sculpturally in several stages. Since 1990 CATIA software, developed in France for use in the automobile and aerospace industry, has been used to translate these complex architectural models into a digital form that can be further manipulated at computer workstations.

It is this process that has virtually revolutionized architecture since then. Now it is possible to quickly and precisely understand even the most complex forms. This allows structural engineers and builders to construct extremely complicated forms economically for the first time in the history of architecture.

This technology makes it possible to translate extreme curves from models into prefabricated building elements. This marks the beginning of a new era in which cost-effective realization of even Gehry's most expressive designs is possible. The legendary American archiect Philip Johnson, the grand eminence of the 20th century's international architectural scene, wryly praised the development as a veritable Pandora's box, saying, "Now everyone knows it's possible to do anything."

Pariser Platz 3, Berlin, Germany, 1994–99

One of Gehry's favorite material mixes: white stuccoed
walls, wood and metal roof surfaces.

Selected Works 1969 to Today

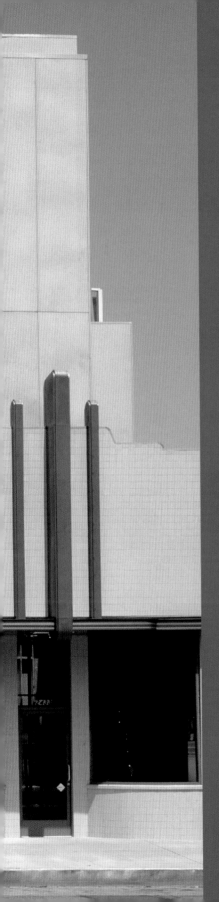

Edgemar Project

Santa Monica, California
1984–1988

New Life for Main Street

The Edgemar Project incorporates spaces for the Santa Monica Museum of Art and commercial uses on the site of a former dairy in downtown Santa Monica. The complex is a collage of the existing industrial buildings combined with autonomous new additions, each with its own individual architectural expression. Together the new and old buildings form a village-like composition that creates human scale and lively urbanity to virtuously reinvigorate this section of Santa Monica's commercially struggling Main Street.

An art deco facade fragment of an existing commercial building forms the focus of the composition on Main Street and marks the entry into the interior courtyard from which shops and museum spaces are accessed. A sculpture-like vertical tower element sheathed in sheet metal that rises above the art deco facade fragment serves as a marker for the new mixed-use complex. The adjacent curving front of shops, also wrapped in sheet metal, forms an inviting gateway to the inner courtyard. The street frontage is augmented by further sheet metal–clad sculptural elements, such as the stair to the parking structure and an office space that create a lively foil to diminish the blank facade of the parking structure behind.

Two more tower elements visible from the street form a dynamic composition together with the street-side tower and lure the visitor into the inner courtyard, from which the museum spaces located in the transformed dairy buildings are accessed.

The first courtyard tower, topped with an open steel framework, marks the transition from street to courtyard and creates an open-air meeting space for the first floor offices. The second courtyard tower, with its glazed top, marks the central courtyard space like a town-hall tower in a medieval town. Together the three tower elements and the piazza-like courtyard underscore and strengthen the allusion to urban patterns common to typical European villages and create a sense of intimate urban scale uncommon in automobile-infatuated Los Angeles.

The inner courtyard serves as the urban focus of the composition and invites one to relax and sit at the café after visiting the shops or the museum spaces located in the revamped former dairy buildings.

The location of the public museum spaces at the rear of the site, unnoticeable from the street, signals a conscious decision to create a new type of museum far removed from the conventional understanding of the museum as an autonomous institution housed in a conventional, solitary building.

As such, this project was one of the first to unite art and commerce functions in a common building complex. This creative mix of uses made it economically feasible to both realize the museum and revitalize the derelict industrial site into a lively urban node in this formerly neglected section of downtown Santa Monica.

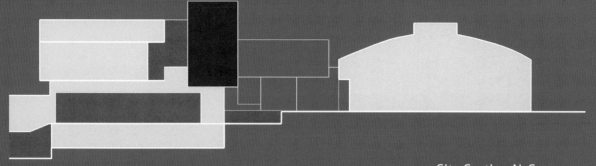

Site Section N–S

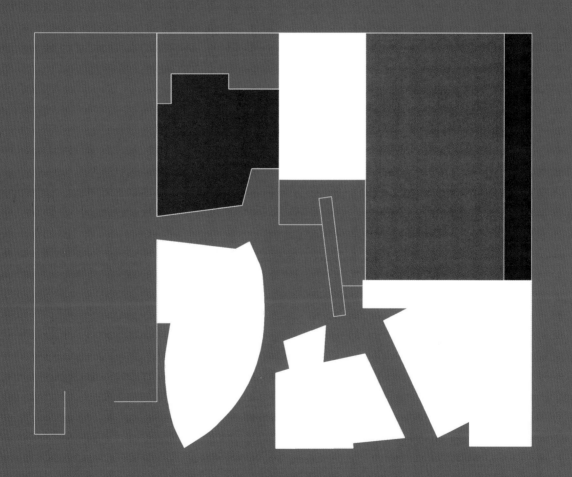

Site Plan

A palette of industrial materials such as zinc-coated metal sheeting, semitransparent wire mesh and exposed concrete was used to give the individual elements of the composition's different characters.

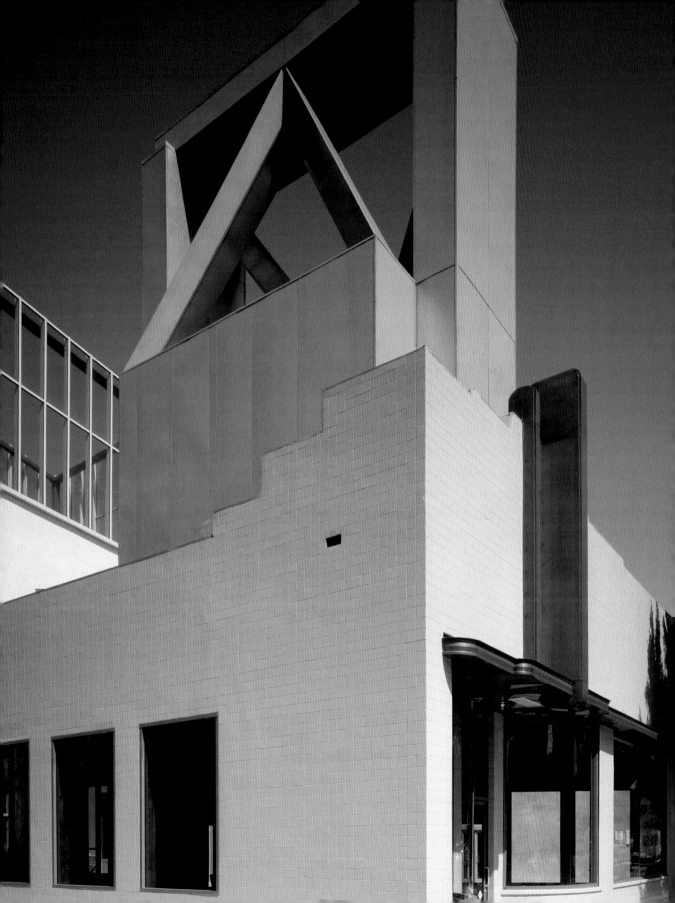

The transformation of a derelict industrial site into a vital node in the inner-city structure was enlivened by the contrast of old with new.

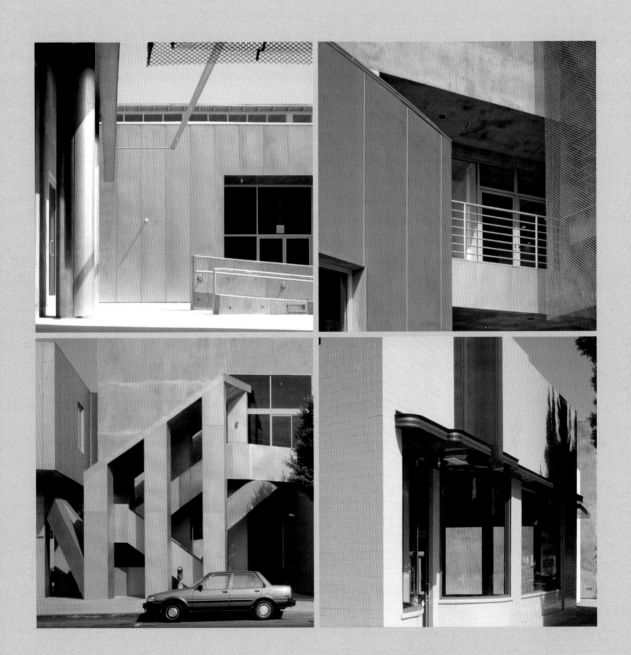

Windows

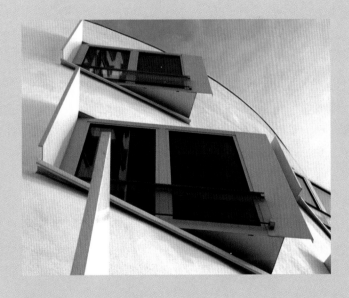

Like a Swarm of Bees

In accordance with Gehry's understanding of architecture as sculptural object, openings in walls and roofs take on an important function that is an absolutely essential key to understanding his design approach. Gehry skillfully deploys windows to modulate and differentiate each individual building's sculpturally composed surfaces and to imbue each of his buildings with its own unique, poetry-like architectural expression.

But sculptors need not deal with the sensitive issue of creating weather-tight architectural window details. Although they can concentrate solely on the pure formal quality of their works, architects must address practical concerns, such as allowing light and air into their buildings and at the same time protecting the interior spaces from the elements. This makes the windows, doors and skylights of Gehry's designs essential elements he not only carefully designs to achieve ingenious architectural details but also creatively deploys to underscore the sculptural intention and address the unique requirements that each design challenge presents.

Gehry's concert halls and museums are often sheathed in continuous metal surfaces with few individual window openings. These largely closed surfaces are often contrasted with generous glass surfaces and unique skylight structures. The resultant extensively glazed window fronts and sculpture-like rooftop skylights augment the organic, soaring, metal-clad forms of Gehry's grand museums and concert halls.

Stata Center, Cambridge, USA, 2000–04

The design of windows for office buildings and residential projects requires a different approach than when creating museums or concert halls since the windows here must provide each individual space with adequate amounts of light and air. In his office buildings and residential projects Gehry therefore emphasizes the individual window elements as modulating devices to underscore the design intention and sculptural quality of each overall building composition.

Tired of accepting the conventional definition of a window as "part of the building skin," Gehry articulates his windows here as sculptural elements that have their own presence, underscore the overall design intention of each specific project and emphasize the requirements, challenges and sculptural intention of each design.

Gehry masterfully composes groups and architectural zones of tilted windows aligned in jazz-like syncopation to create the impression that they seem to fly like "a swarm of bees coming at a wall." Gehry's windows are consciously and clearly shifted out of the facades and emphasized as autonomous elements.

Rather than plodding along in conventionality, Gehry developed his unique approach to designing window compositions, which he himself sums up as follows: "I worked very hard trying to devise a window that looked like it was attacking the form instead of eating it away."

Pariser Platz 3, Berlin, Germany, 1994–99

The windows of Pariser Platz 3 in Berlin
resemble a "swarm of bees that hit the building."

Bard Theater, Annandale, USA, 2000–03

Disney Hall in Los Angeles (1988–2003):
The perforated windows of the street-side
wing contrast with the open foyer glazing.

Vitra Design Museum

Weil am Rhein, Germany
1987–1989

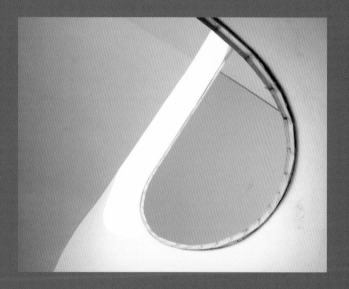

Design on the Rhine

This building, which serves as an exhibition space for the Vitra Furniture Company at its headquarters outside the town of Weil am Rhein in southern Germany, near the Swiss border, was Gehry's premiere in Europe, a continent where he thereafter created a major body of his most important works. This commission offered Gehry his first opportunity to create a design for the European context and was his first project to be built in Europe. Gehry's design strategy, which had been perfected and experimented with in his earlier American projects, was honed to perfection for his first European commission.

By exploring and redefining the boundaries between sculpture and architectural structure the Vitra Design Museum immediately set a new, quite difficult to meet, standard for all new museums worldwide. From its date of completion on, the Vitra Design Musuem has had a major influence on all major museum projects that have been built since.

Clearly, the formal canon Gehry described here continues to live on as one of the world's architectural highlights of the late 1980s and has informed and influenced countless other projects and designs since. The essential message Gehry communicates with his Vitra Design Museum composition is that architecture can boldly merge with sculpture to transcend the box-like drabness of so much modernist architecture. This creative, dynamic approach offers an alternative to the austerity of poetic minimalism that continues to fascinate architects and their clients up to this day.

The architect's affinity for art and his long-standing close relationship with artists is boldly evident in this composition. The building itself is conceived as a veritable sculpture that stands in dialogue with the tool gate sculpture piece by Claes Oldenburg and Coosje van Bruggen. As a memorable icon the building plays a major role in defining Vitra's corporate identity.

The expressive handling, and even distortion, of the white stucco building volumes — the stairwell as snail, skylights and entrance roof as oblique boxes — creates a collage building that turns the modernist paradigm "form follows function" inside out, without negating it. This concerted explosion of forms is unified through the reduction of materials used on the exterior: stucco over masonry and titanium-zinc roofing panels.

The cubist pavilion goes beyond conventional museum concepts by hosting exhibitions on design history and current trends in international design. The complex also houses a library, offices, shops and storage space.

The exhibition spaces are interconnected but can also be used separately. Each memorable interior space emanates a specific ambience underscored by varied natural light, individual scale, textured surface and distinctive spatial composition within the whole.

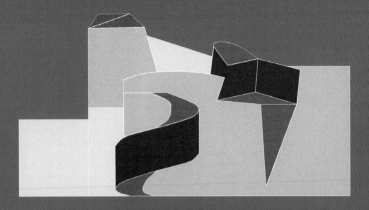

South Elevation

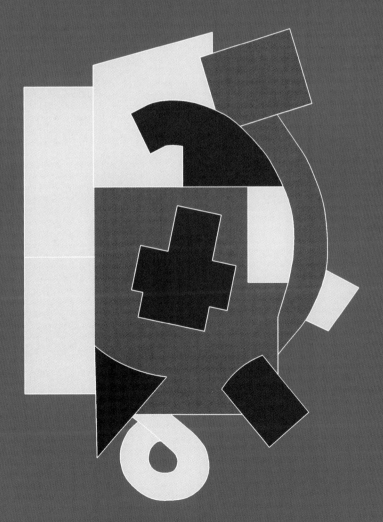

Roof Plan

Each side of the building was individually designed in order to allow it to appear as a built sculpture from the outside and to create variegated spaces inside.

The expressive handling of the building volumes turns the modernist
paradigm "form follows function" inside out, without negating it.

The building's back elevation serves as a reserved backdrop for the explosive composition.

The poured-concrete building forms were foreseen with plaster exterior surfaces. Zinc-coated metal was used as the exterior roof material.

The tool gate sculpture
by Claes Oldenburg and
Coosje van Bruggen.

The spiral stair that leads up to the upper exhibition level forms the focus of the composition on the south side.

Gehry "punches" holes out of the roof surfaces to carefully direct natural light into the interior exhibition spaces.

Blue-painted wire mesh hung from the ceiling creates a cool contrast to the
warm materials — wood flooring and white plaster walls — used in the interiors.

The interconnected
exhibition spaces each
emanate a specific ambience
underscored by varied
natural light.

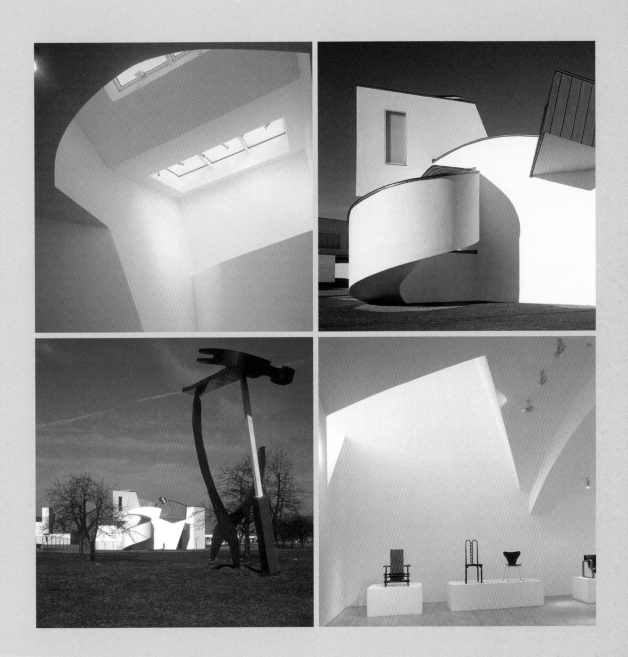

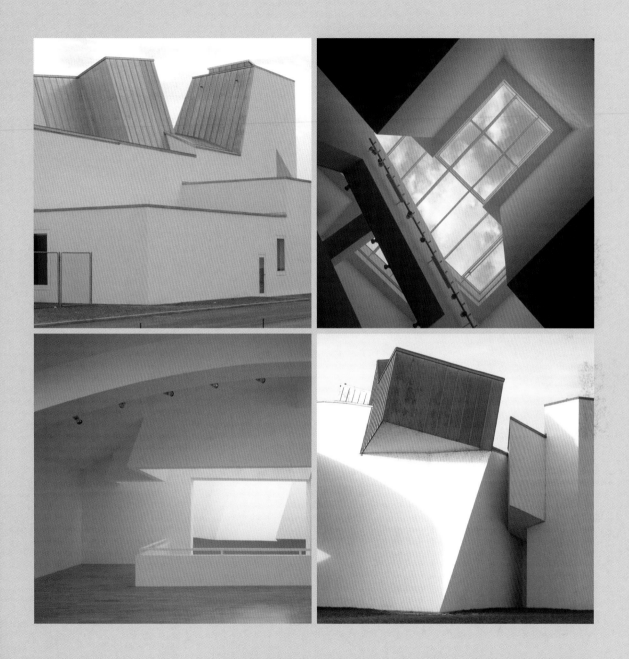

Edges Furniture

Easy Edges 1969–1973
Experimental Edges 1979–1982

Making Something from Nothing

Gehry's inquisitive search for new ways of approaching conventional design challenges and achieving creative new solutions is by no means limited to the "mere" realm of architecture.

The creation of the "ideal chair," an age-old challenge that has confronted generations of architects, designers and furniture builders, also whets his insatiable creative appetite. And in addition to rising to meet the theoretical design challenge of creating an "ideal chair," the chairs of Gehry's Easy Edges furniture series (1969–73) were conceived to be especially affordable and mass-producible and therefore available to a broad consumer market not only interested in design objects but also concerned mainly with buying attractive and especially affordable furniture.

Using cardboard, a material that until then led a dull life as packaging material destined to soon land on the nearest garbage heap, Gehry created a new material for furniture construction that he deemed "edgeboard." By cross-laminating the individual cardboard layers, a new furniture material was created that has the color, a perceived warmth and a structural strength surprisingly similar to real wood.

In comparison with wood, "edgeboard" is easy to work with and inexpensive and has the added advantage that it can be made with renewable resources and recycled paper products.

But after the first production phase of the Easy Edges furniture series was complete Gehry was faced with the financial realities of the project and a major decision that would play a major role in his future career: Should he give up architecture to pursue the furniture business? After difficult perusal of the possibilities and potentials offered he decided to stick with his "day job" as an architect and the Easy Edges series was taken out of production.

Nonetheless, the challenge of creating the "ideal chair" continued to intrigue Gehry's creative mind. Six years after the Easy Edges series went out of the first production phase Gehry conceived the Experimental Edges series (1979–82), also fabricated in cardboard. For this series prefabricated cardboard panels typically used to make doors were glued together to create comfortably generous easy chairs.

Gehry's ever-increasing notoriety led to increased international demand for his unique furniture designs. Originally conceived as furniture for a broad market, the original Easy Edges series went back into production to meet the demand presented by an increasingly design-conscious clientele.

In the meantime, both the Easy Edges and Experimental Edges series have achieved status as design icons beloved by clients around the world. Both series are currently manufactured by Vitra International.

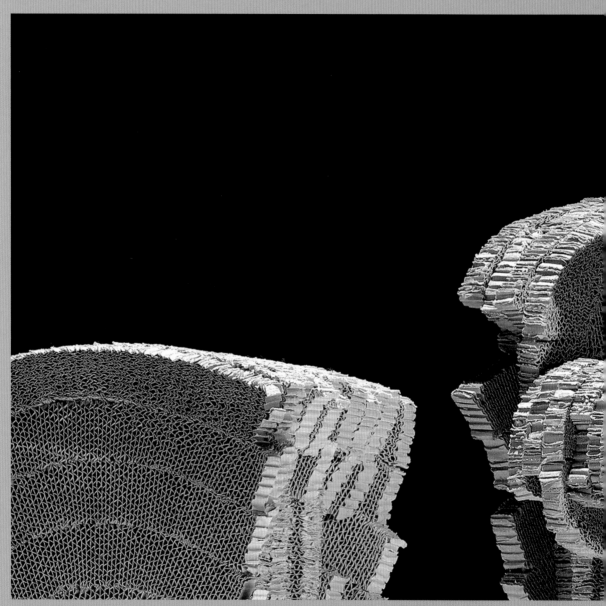

Experimental Edges, Easy Chair, 1979–82

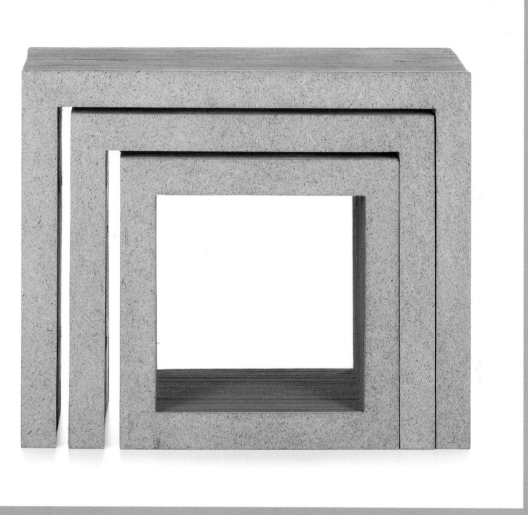

Gehry uses cardboard to form "edgeboard" for the
Easy Edges furniture series.

Edgeboard has color, warmth and strength surprisingly
similar to wood.

The clear forms of the Easy Edges series are also a result of the originally envisioned broad market for the furniture as an inexpensive, mass-produced consumer product.

American Center

Paris, France
1988–1994

Étude Parisienne

The American Center, a long-standing Parisian institution located in Montparnasse from 1931 to 1987, asked Gehry to design their ambitious new mixed-use complex to enliven a derelict, former industrial site in Paris located not far from another major project of the era, the French National Library.

Gehry rose to the challenge of creating human scale, urbanity and cultural density in the derelict location with his design for a complex that respects the omnipresent Parisian urban and architectural traditions without emulating or capitulating to them.

Sensibly reacting to the special nature of the French capital, the architect uses a palette of traditional Parisian materials to sculpt his unique composition. Limestone, glass and zinc building masses form Gehry's "petite ville full of dance and music and energy like the city ... an American interpretation of Paris as I see it, without trying to make a French building."

Skillfully sited to create urbanity and density on the former industrial site, the building creates a convincing, confident, urban statement that interconnects well with the surrounding residential quarters and reinvigorates this section of the Parisian urban fabric with lively cultural and residential functions.

The 198,000 square foot complex was conceived to host a broad range of uses. The main entrance in the southwest corner fronts directly on the new Parc Bercy urban landscape park. The entrance leads to the open central hall, around which various public functions, such as multipurpose performance, rehearsal and exhibition spaces, a bookstore, a restaurant and the 400-seat theater, are oriented.

Further uses, including exhibition spaces for temporary and permanent exhibitions, various office zones, apartments for visiting artists and residents, an integrated language school and various studios for artists and dance classes, are vertically stacked on the upper floors.

Despite the Center's popularity and high numbers of visitors the American Center's ambitious program could not generate the funds needed to remain open. After only 19 months of operation it closed as an institution in the winter of 1996, and the building was put up for sale.

But Gehry's spatial concept proved readily flexible to easily accommodate new uses. In October 2003 renovation work began for the new Musée du Cinéma der Cinémathéque Francais. This institution that celebrates French cinema has since filled the building with new, lasting life to demonstrate that the virtuosity and creativity inherent in Gehry's designs can be effectively adapted to meet new requirements and challenges.

Ground Floor

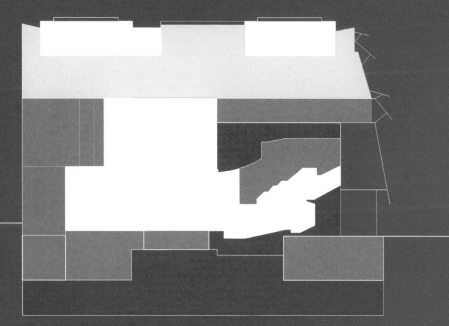

Theater Section

"A petite ville full of dance and music and energy like the city. It is an American interpretation of Paris as I see it, without trying to make a French building."

Vila Olimpica

Barcelona, Spain
1989–1992

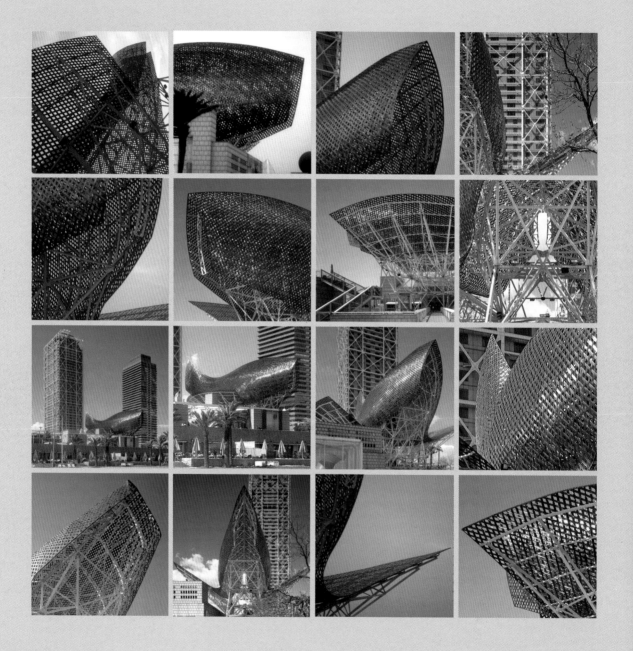

Fish and Games

Located on the beachfront in Barcelona's 1992 Olympic Village, Gehry's complex creates an important commercial node for a vital new urban quarter and plays a central role in the successful urban revitalization that has occurred on this section of Barcelona's beachfront in the ensuing years since the 1992 Olympics.

Nestled between a hotel tower and the lively Paseo Maritimo beach promenade, this 150,000 square foot retail center provides an exuberant focus within the surrounding new urban fabric and celebrates the beachfront site with a convincing composition of shopping, office and commercial spaces.

The required buildings housing these functions define clear urban spaces that accommodate the warm Barcelona climate and create inviting outdoor spaces that can be used throughout the changing seasons.

A variety of elements were used to define these special public urban spaces. Bridges and trellises form inviting outdoor spaces on the promenade for street cafes open year round. The urban spaces formed between the buildings and the urban beachfront promenade were clearly defined and articulated through skillful allocation of the building masses and the secondary space-defining sculptural elements, such as the fish sculpture and the shade-spending pergolas.

A mesh-covered fish sculpture serves as the memorable focal point of the composition and serves a variety of purposes. In addition to serving as an evocative landmark and trademark for the complex, its expressive form imbues a playful lightness evocative of the Mediterranean that effectively contrasts with the rational aesthetic of the hotel tower and other austere modernist buildings nearby. The wire-mesh sculpture also offers much needed cooling shade for the outdoor retail court with its sun-protected café seating areas.

Gehry had long been fascinated by the fish motif and explored it in several earlier projects — most notably the Fish Dance Restaurant in Kobe, Japan (1986–87), the Fish Lamp (1983–86), the GFT Fish in Turin (1985–86) — but whereas the fish sculpture of the Fish Dance Restaurant was designed using then conventional hand-drafting methods, the Vila Olimpica project marks the first use of computer 3D modeling technology in his office's design practice and therefore marks a major new point of departure in Gehry's trajectory.

Starting with this project, he discovered and increasingly employed CATIA, French software originally developed for aircraft design. This proved to be a crucial development in Gehry's rise to international prominence. The extremely complex forms of his ever-larger commissions from 1990 on could henceforth be made understandable, cost-efficient and startlingly realistic.

The new beach promenade as the center of Barcelona's Olympic Village.

Starting with this project, Gehry increasingly employed CATIA software.
Henceforth, complex forms could be made cost-efficient and suddenly realistic.

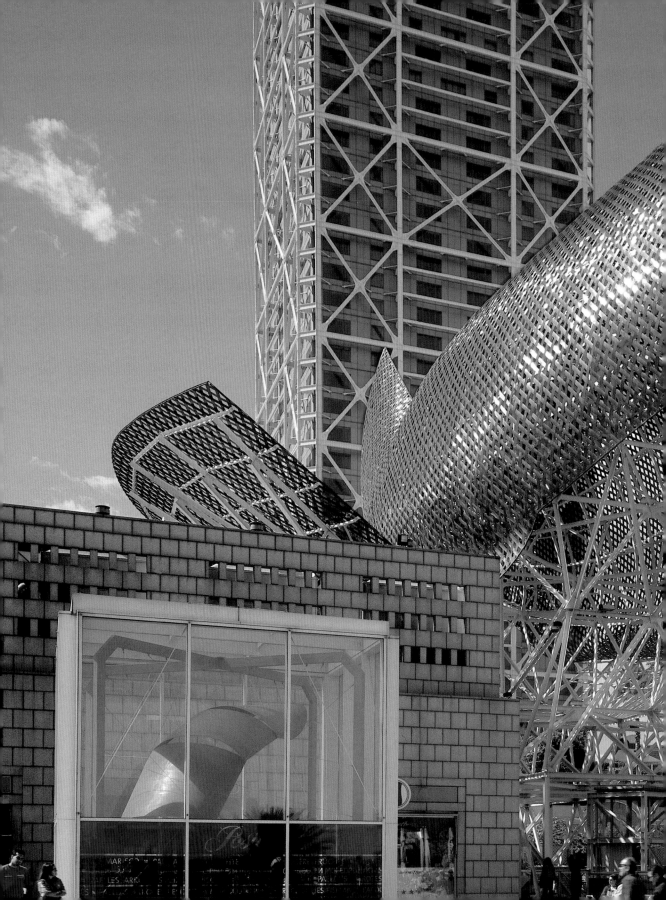

The expressive form of the fish sculpture imbues a lightness evocative of the Mediterranean and contrasts with the rational aesthetic of the surroundings.

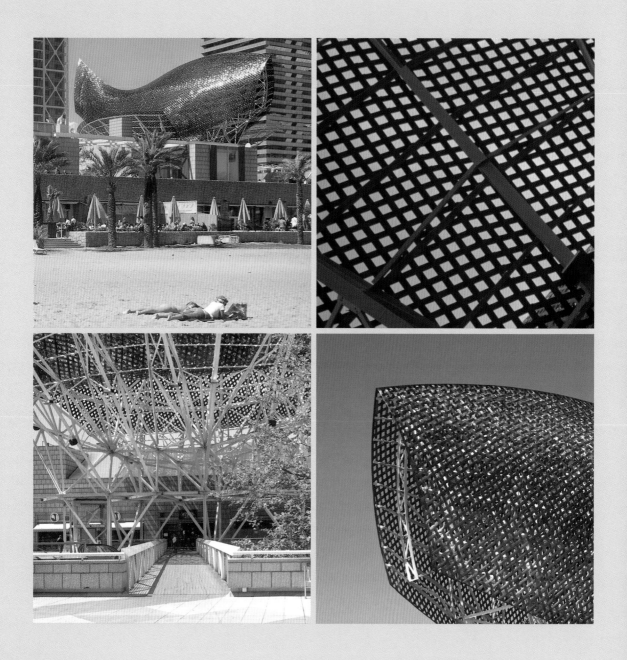

Building with Metal

Building with Metal

Around the mid-1970s metal becomes one of the essential elements that enrich Gehry's architecture and enhance its sculptural quality. It is metal's potential to take on different qualities in changing light conditions that especially fascinates the architect and leads him to develop new ways of employing it and also to search for ever better metal materials that elevate the complex sculptural compositions to ephemeral objects that seem either to surrealistically hover above the ground or merge with the skies above.

Corrugated sheet metal was one of the earliest metals used to sheathe his own house in Santa Monica, as well as the Spiller residence in Venice and many other early projects. This prototypical American material was well suited to underscoring Gehry's initial exploration of "junk architecture" when he started out on his creative new redefinition of architecture after distancing himself from the then-prevalent late modernism of 1960s Los Angeles. Gehry elevated the "junk" material, commonly used on sheds, as well as for industrial and military complexes, to poetic status by using it like a quip on American culture in unexpected ways and contexts.

Gehry similarly employed chain-link fencing, usually in the simplest form available — silver, zinc-coated wire mesh — in his further creative experimentation with "junk" materials, especially since this inexpensive chain-link fencing is used

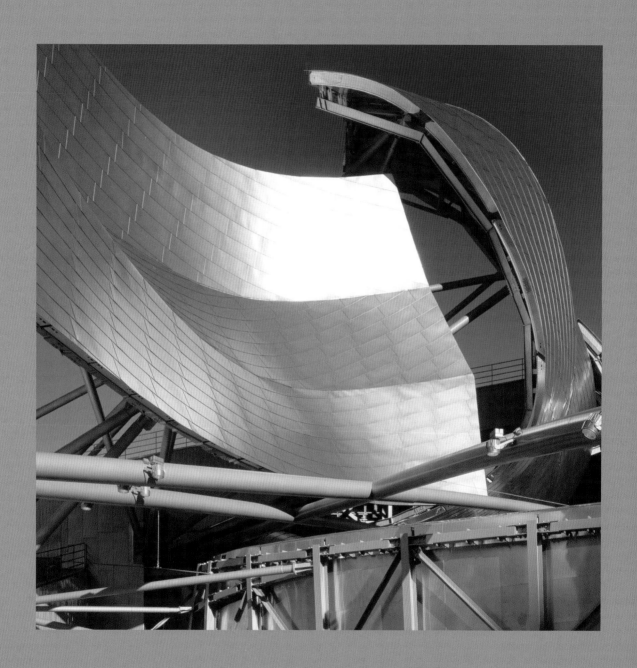

everywhere in Los Angeles to construct high fences to guard against burglars. Says Gehry, "I had to use the stuff near every building I was doing so I decided to make it part of the architecture."

He used chain link to veil entire building elements, appearing sometimes transparent and sometimes as closed surfaces, according to the light available. This ambivalence helps his architecture increasingly jump the barrier between art and architecture. Gehry's fascination with this material found its culmination in the projects of the late 1970s, such as the Santa Monica Place Shopping Mall (1972–80), where he used chain-link fencing on the entire southern facade of the 1,000-place, multilevel parking structure, or at the Cabrillo Marine Museum (1977–79), where it was employed to create light, airy roofs for the outdoor circulation spaces.

Zinc metal sheeting is increasingly used to differentiate the elements in Gehry's sculptural compositions from the 1980s on. Gehry's commission for the Sheet Metal Craftsmanship exhibition at the National Building Museum (1986–88) documents the architect's fascination with and command of this material. From the late 1980s until today, titanium and stainless steel have become two of the architect's signature materials, the use of which depends upon the natural light prevalent at each site. For example, whereas in gray Bilbao, gold-shimmering titanium panels were employed to lighten the building's ambience, stainless steel panels that appear white in the stark Southern California sunshine were used to wrap the Disney Concert Hall.

Pariser Platz 3, Berlin, Germany, 1994–99

The use of metal is further refined in the buildings built after 2000. Metal "shingles" were used to clad the BP Bridge in Chicago, whereas the roofs in Herford were foreseen as smooth, shimmering surfaces.

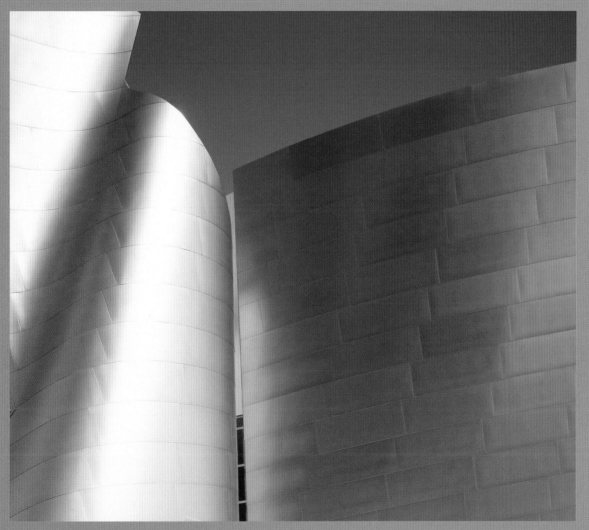

The metal used is chosen with respect to the special nature of light at each site. The stainless steel of the Disney Concert Hall glows white in the California sun.

Millennium Park, Chicago, USA, 1999-2004

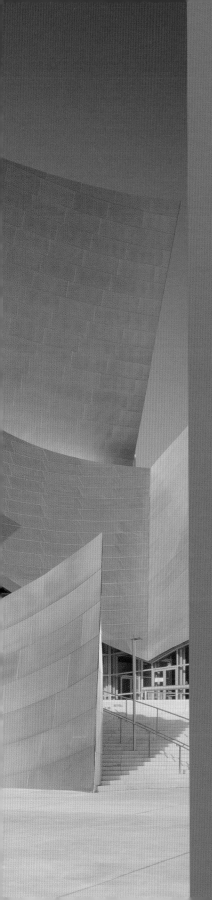

Disney Concert Hall

Los Angeles, California
1988–2003

Like Pulsating Music

For decades, Los Angeles' downtown was the city's alarmingly neglected urban problem child, with high crime levels, a constantly falling residential population and a deteriorated commercial situation that made it scarcely attractive for new businesses or corporations to locate here. Seen in this light, Gehry's Disney Concert Hall provided dynamic impetus for the revitalization of this important, long-forgotten inner-city quarter of one of America's most vibrant metropolises.

Gehry's bold statement has acted as a veritable urban magnet for the renewal of the Grand Street district and attracted countless tourists and, more importantly, Los Angelenos back into the inner city.

But the ambitious cultural complex wasn't easy to realize: it required 30,000 drawings and 16 years of planning and construction before it was completed in 2003. Gehry responded to the difficult challenge of solving the pressing urban problems outside and at the same time creating an ambience conducive to use by philharmonic orchestras inside and herewith convincingly completed his largest cultural building commission to date in his hometown.

The shiny titanium skin of the towering structure catches the Southern California sunlight and reflects it into a shady public park at its base that has become a beloved green oasis in the midst of the concrete and asphalt of the surrounding vicinity.

Contrary to the first impression, the seemingly chaotic building masses are anything but coincidental. Since the 2,265-seat main hall was designed first, it generated the location of the adjoining building wings and their shapes. After the appropriate form for the hall was found, the rest of the building elements were skillfully grouped around its central volume — Gehry calls this "designing from the inside out."

As the focus of the composition, the reverence of the hall's interior stands in marked contrast to the ecstatic celebration of forms on the exterior. Mezzanines and tiers are wrapped all around the concert hall space, allowing the orchestra to stand virtually in the center of the grand space.

Paneled on all surfaces in vibrant Douglas fir, the interior surfaces in the concert hall seem natural and warm and effectively contrast with the cool metal surfaces outside. The disposition of the main concert hall with the central stage ensures a good view of the orchestra from every seat and gives the hall exceptional acoustics that satisfy both the demanding musicians of the LA Philharmonic and the ever-critical concert-going public.

YOU ARE
PARKED ON
3B
MARK YOUR TICKET

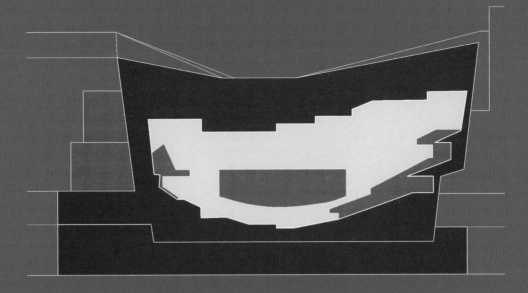

Theater Section

Roof Plan

The new Disney Concert Hall complex provides dynamic impetus for the revitalization of this important inner-city quarter.

The buildings reflect the sunlight into the cool shade of the city park.

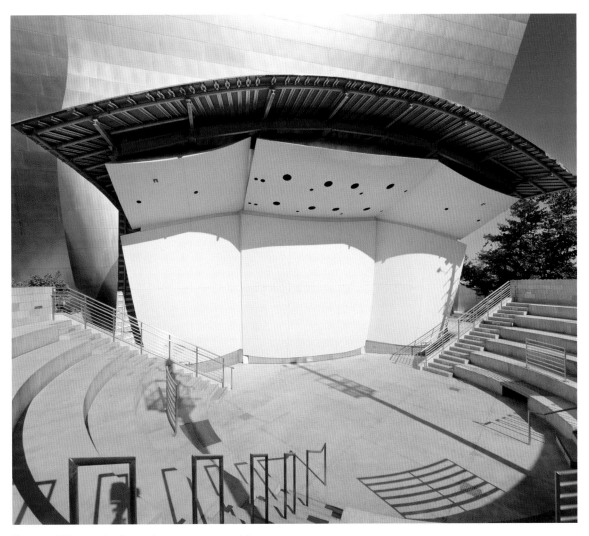

The amphitheater in the park serves as an outdoor
concert venue.

In the foyer, wood panels form a warming contrast to the cool metal surfaces on the exterior.

The foyers offer concertgoers ample space to take an intermezzo on several levels during the concert intermission.

One of the focuses in the hall itself is formed by the imposing
organ sculpture.

As places of reflection within the building, these spaces receive natural light from skylights, which imbue them with a mystical, almost sacred quality.

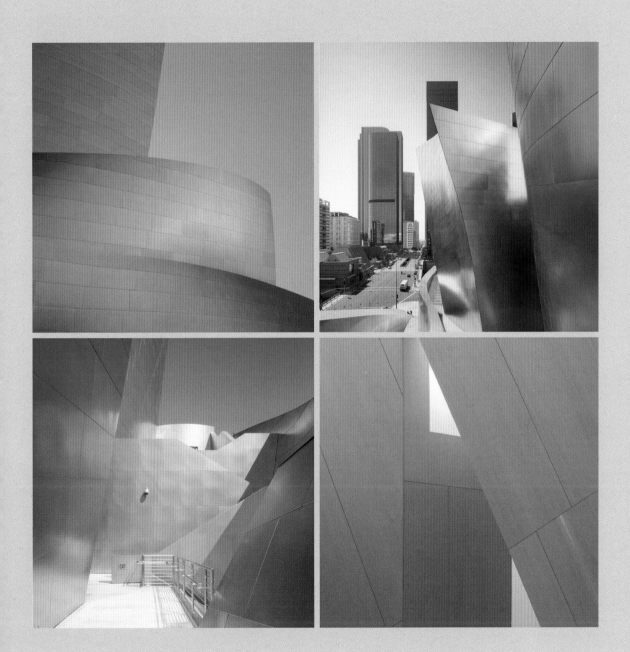

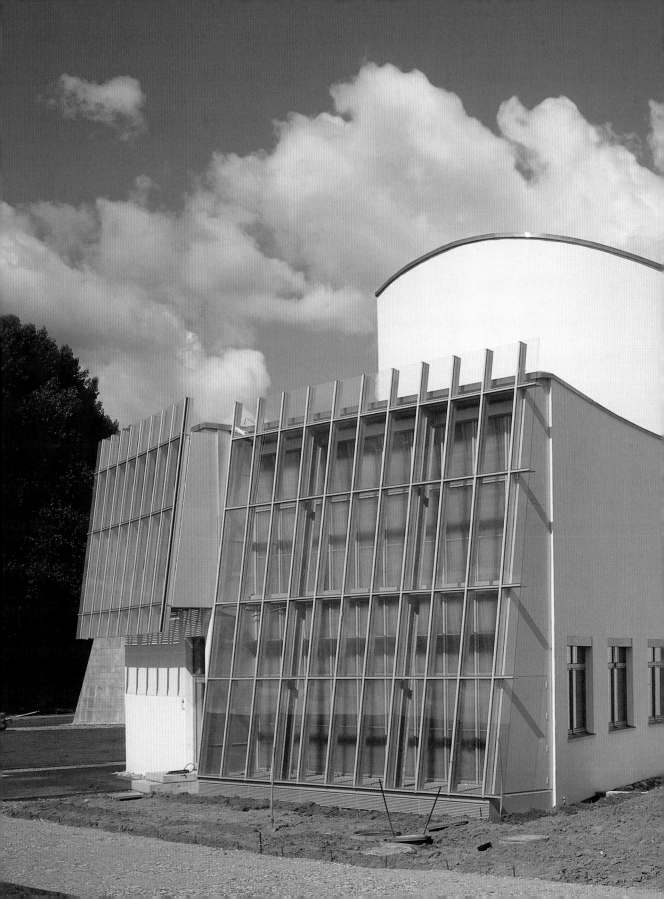

EMR Center

Bad Oeynhausen, Germany
1991–1995

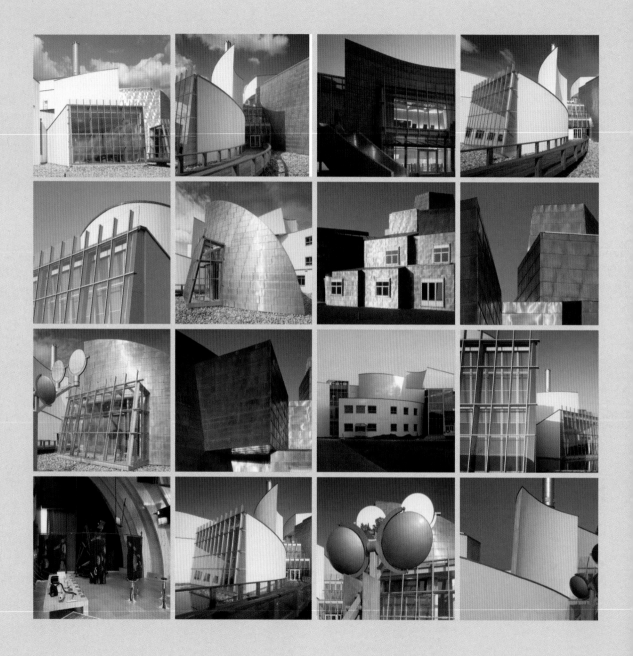

Energetic Activity

To augment an ambitious public relations program, to increase understanding in the general public for their energy company and to promote energy conservation, the EMR (Elektrizitätswerk Minden-Ravensberg GmbH) asked Gehry to design their new communication and technology center in Bad Oeynhausen as his second major commission in Germany after the Vitra Design Museum.

Located alongside a major traffic artery that passes through the small town, the 43,000 square foot complex contains an exhibition hall where school classes and interested visitors can learn how a modern power company operates as its main focal space. An important goal of the facility is to provide an overview of the complicated nature of energy production in today's society. A strong emphasis is placed on furthering sustainable energy technologies and improving consumer behavior to conserve energy and natural resources.

Gehry therefore translated the client's program requirements into a poetic sculptural ensemble composed of interconnected yet separate building elements. This allowed the allocation of the various required program areas in unique building wings that were each foreseen with an individual character.

A carefully determined palette of materials was used to enhance this strategy: white stucco rendering, large glazed surfaces and metal sheeting were used to clad the various building wings and allow them to appear as autonomous parts that express individuality and create a village-like sense of scale well suited to the small German town.

But the architect also skillfully combines all the diverse parts to create a coherent whole, enabling the new building to act as a memorable "city gate" on Bad Oeynhausen's eastern edge and defining a clear urban street-space that transforms the bland traffic artery into an attractive urban place that asserts itself convincingly against the nondescript surroundings on the outskirts of the town.

The office and technical facilities are sited in linear building wings parallel to the street that underscore and define the street-front. The individual pavilions behind the street-front wing sensitively relate to the surrounding context and open out to the Werre River and the nearby ridge of the Wiehe Mountains to the north.

Roof Plan

Section

The building is conceived to convey the progressive goals of the public
utility company to a broad public.

The building parts are
handled in different
materials to create an
ensemble of autonomous
architectural elements.

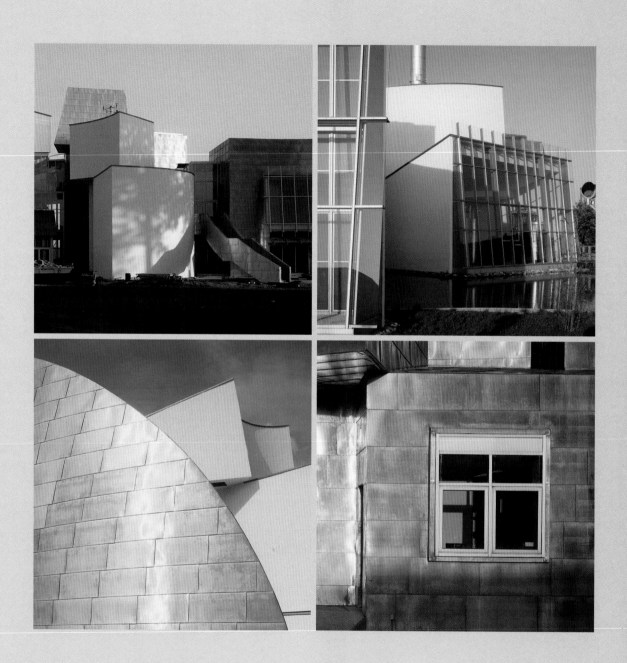

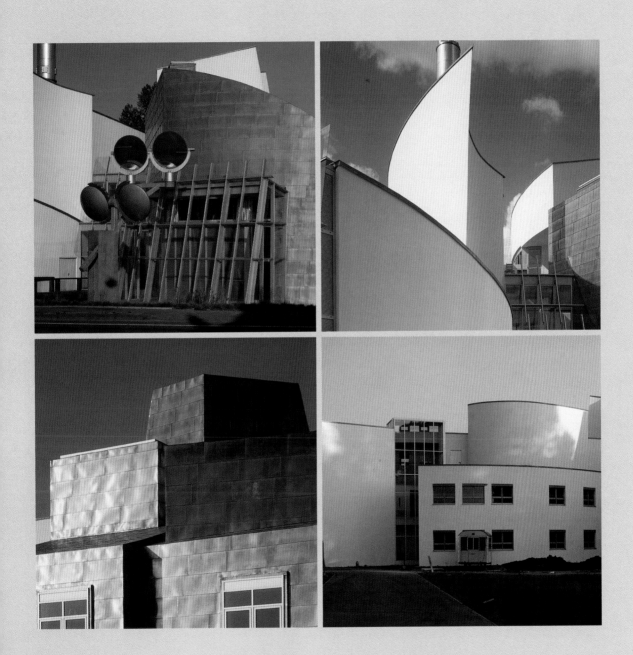

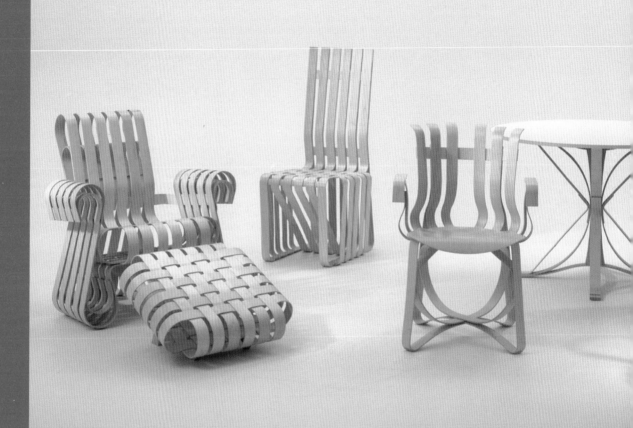

Bentwood Furniture

Knoll International
1989–1992

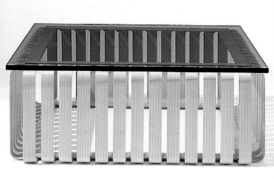

Hat Trick

By the end of the 1970s Gehry had already begun design of a new kind of lightweight wood furniture with the intention of overcoming the conventional separation between support elements and the actual seating surface that has characterized almost all chair designs throughout time.

And Gehry was still concerned with the notion of creating something meaningful, elegant and creative using everyday materials commonly used for other functions, such as the wooden slats of apple crates that Gehry remembered seeing while growing up in his native Canada before moving to Southern California to study architecture at the University of Southern California in the 1950s.

After thinking about the potentials for such a new, revolutionary chair design for several years, the Knoll International Furniture Company set up a workshop right next to Gehry's Santa Monica studio in 1989, allowing him to work intensely on the innovative design with skilled woodworkers on a day-to-day, hands-on basis and turn his visionary ideas into the reality of the popular Bentwood furniture series that has been successfully manufactured by Knoll International since 1992.

Attempting to create a simple yet innovative chair in wood and go beyond the conventional understanding of chairs with separate legs, seats and backs, Gehry said he didn't want to just "hang another coat on four legs and a seat."

Drawing inspiration from traditional wicker furniture and the wooden apple crates he had played on in childhood, Gehry designed a furniture collection that he humorously named after terms common in ice hockey. Wafer-thin strips of laminated wood were ingeniously bent, woven and curled into fluid, featherweight, yet extremely sturdy forms.

It was a groundbreaking idea that met with immediate accolades from both Knoll customers and the professional community. The Museum of Modern Art in New York — always at the vanguard of the design and architectural discussion — displayed production samples in a museum window show before the chairs were even released to the public.

The furniture is constructed of hard white maple veneers in 2 inch wide strips that are laminated with high-bonding glue. All wood grains run in the same direction for resilience. Thermo-set assembly glue provides structural rigidity without the need for metal connectors, while allowing for ergonomic movement and flexibility. The backs of all chairs flex for added comfort.

The underside of each piece is embossed with Gehry's signature and the date of the chair's production.

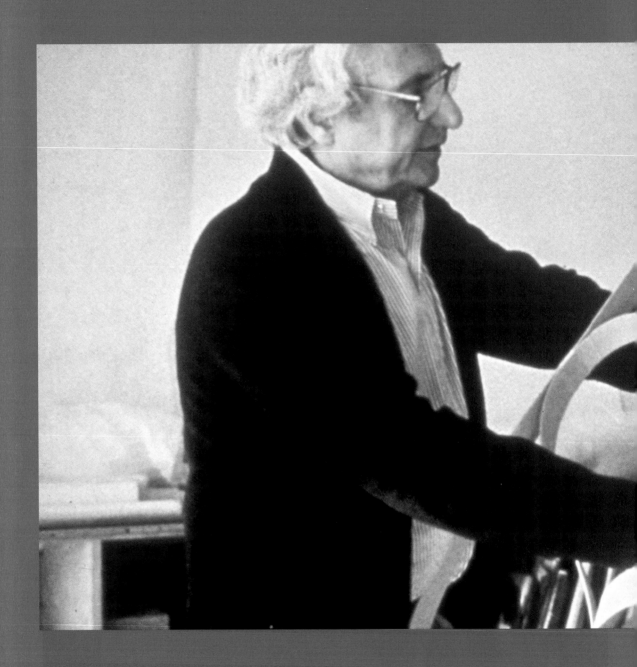

The furniture manufacturer Knoll
International outfitted a wood
shop near Gehry's California
offices to provide him with the
relaxed atmosphere conducive
to the creative design process.

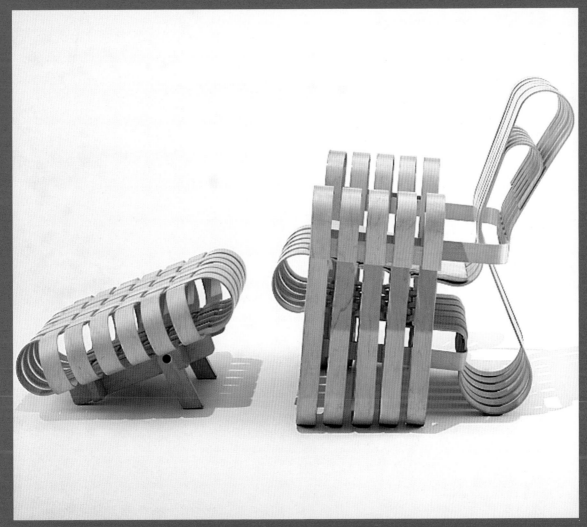

Drawing inspiration from the apple crates he had played on in childhood, Gehry employs laminated maple strips to create the Bentwood furniture series.

Gehry sought to overcome the conventional separation between support elements and the actual seating surface.

The furniture is suited to both office and home use.

Goldstein Housing

Frankfurt, Germany
1991–1996

A Different Housing Project

Gehry's colorful buildings extend an existing 1960s housing project west of Frankfurt, Germany, to create an unconventional and playful contrast to the bland anonymity of the neighboring high-rise social housing projects that deface the nearby cityscape on the urban periphery of one of southern Germany's largest cities.

Two distinct building groups clearly define neighborhoods to the north and south. Street identification is ensured and emphasized as inhabitants have their "own," unique house — in spite of the large project's total 162 housing units that cover over 110,000 square feet.

The architect's wise design decision to create two distinct neighborhoods that increase user identification is followed through right on down to the smallest detail of the individual buildings.

Although the housing blocks are composed of only a few basic types, they are skillfully varied and never repeat the mistakes of the neighboring buildings to become monotonous or repetitive.

through an array of creative design strategies. The building heights are adeptly varied to break down the building masses into identifiable parts.

These well-scaled parts are further delineated by the use of various exterior materials, such as colored stucco rendering and metal sheeting, to increase the sense of human scale and attention to giving each house its own individual character. Splashes of vibrant color — in clear, red, yellow and white tones — help increase the sense of variety and reduce monotony. Zinc metal sheeting is used both to clad entire houses and to accentuate individual balconies and entrance bays and create special design situations uncommon in social housing projects.

Each "neighborhood" is additionally oriented around a central formal element such as the evocative, metal-clad laundry facility with its unique curvilinear forms.

The park landscape, meandering diagonally from north to south across the courtyards, is strongly varied in order to create individual spatial compositions in each neighborhood. In the northern quarter the trees form a perforated natural wall that completes the U-shaped court. The southern quarter boasts an oval green common space that connects to the adjoining public park to the south.

The new buildings create an unconventional, almost playful contrast to the bland anonymity of the neighboring 1960s high-rises.

Site Plan

Although composed
of just a few repeating
basic types, the buildings
are not monotonous.

Guggenheim Bilbao

Bilbao, Spain
1991–1997

Urban Metaphor

Once a decaying industrial city, Bilbao took on new verve with this stunning composition for a Guggenheim museum on a former derelict industrial site. Gehry's creation drew 1.3 million visitors to northern Spain in its first year. It also spawned countless imitators worldwide, all of whom sought to emulate its popularity, aptly dubbed the "Bilbao effect." Seen in this light, this design achieved immediate cult status and will be remembered as one of the 1990s most influential and impressive buildings.

The sculptural virtuosity of forms that Gehry achieved in his design for the Vitra Design Museum in Weil am Rhein, Germany, three years before the Guggenheim Bilbao was conceived was further developed and refined here. Whereas the Vitra museum was designed using then conventional drafting techniques, the Bilbao museum was realized with CATIA software — advanced modeling technology that made realization of the complex forms feasible and affordable.

Where run-down factories once created an urban wasteland blighting the old town, the Guggenheim now mirrors the heavens in its sculptural metal forms. The museum hereby creates a spectacular futuristic contrast, but it also reacts sensitively to the historic urban surroundings of the adjacent old port town. The building skillfully culminates Calle Iparraguire street in an urban plaza that steps down 16 meters to integrate with the waters of the Nervion River before they flow into the nearby Atlantic Ocean.

From the urban plaza at the end of the street a grand urban stairway leads downward to the main entrance from which the central atrium is accessed. This central space accesses a total of 19 diverse exhibition halls containing 11,000 square meters of exhibition space. Upon arrival in the atrium the visitor's eye wanders inexplicably upward to the twisting skylight to discover the source of the warm natural light that makes the atrium space feel so inviting and gracious.

Ten of the exhibition halls are composed of orthogonally organized galleries housed in limestone-clad building wings. These regularly shaped building wings form an urban plinth for the explosion of organic forms that characterize the upper galleries. Sheathed in shiny titanium panels, the sculptural forms of these exhibition spaces stand in marked contrast to the orthogonal plinth. In spite of their expressive, organic forms these galleries serve well as flexible spaces for temporary exhibitions.

With the Bilbao Guggenheim Gehry deservedly emerged internationally as the world's most eminent architect of the 1990s. His unswerving dedication to architecture as an expressive art form founded in modern art and sculpture, especially in the work of Gehry's artist friends such as Jasper Johns and Claes Oldenburg, came into exuberant fruition with this seminal work that not only creates dynamic spaces for viewing art but also at the same time executes a grand urban repair of a struggling city that has since, largely as a result of this successful building, seen a veritable renaissance — a phenomenon that has been further developed by countless cities with memorable "landmark" buildings that

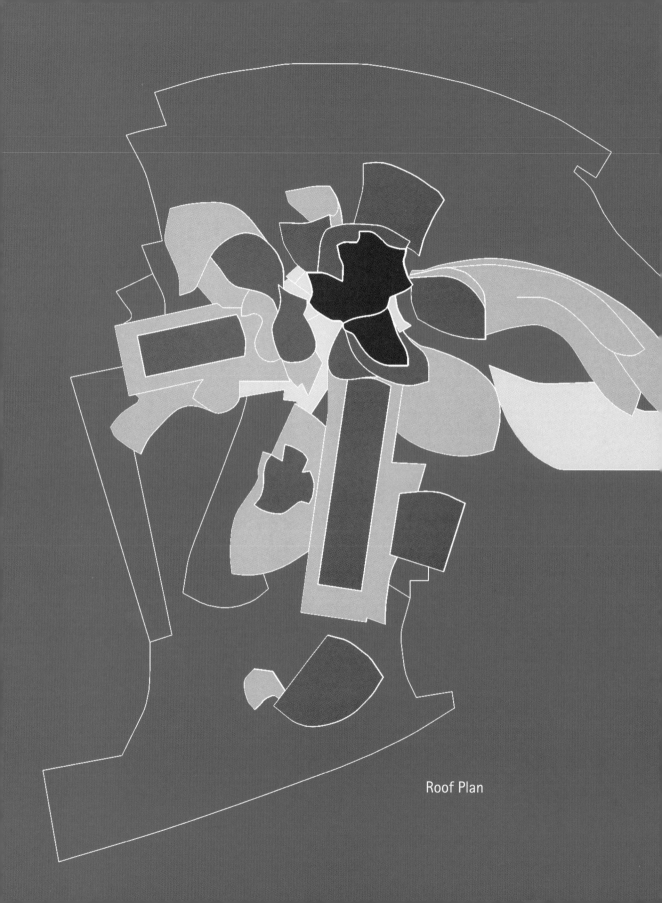

Roof Plan

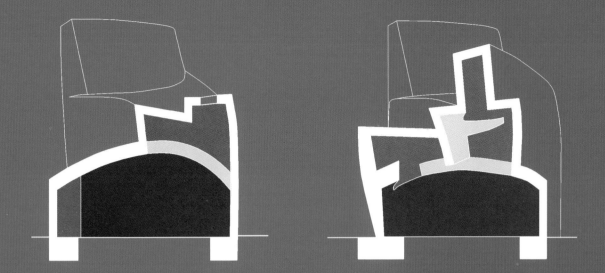

Sections

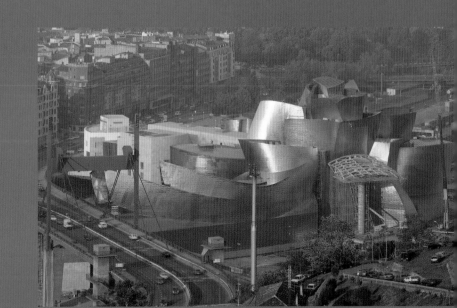

Where run-down factories once created an urban wasteland, the new museum now mirrors the heavens in its sculptural forms.

The museum translates the topography of the nearby hills into built form.

At twilight the building merges with the sky to assume a new identity.

Shiny titanium surfaces reflect the often-gray Bilbao light.

The expressive forms
of the exhibition halls
allow surprisingly flexible
accommodation of varied uses.

Natural Light

Natural Light

When he designed one of his early formative projects, the Danziger House and Studio in Hollywood (1964–65), Gehry "punched" a hole out of the ceiling to create a mixture of the cold northern light from the window with the warm light of the sky above.

Here Gehry carefully alternated completely closed wall and roof surfaces with generous glazed surfaces to create a dramatic light composition that underscored the function of the double-height studio space. Already at this early stage his ability to direct natural light into his buildings to make them warm, uplifting and inviting is clearly evident.

When working with natural light, Gehry — proceeding similarly as he does when conceiving his building compositions — works in a rational and thoughtful way that is at the same time spontaneous and instinctive.

His control and feel for directing light of various qualities into spaces from just the right direction is one of the guiding principles that unites all his best works: "I don't know what I do. I just "punch" a few holes here and there and … they somehow end up being in the right place. I can't say this is what I was trying to do, and this is what I did. I started out to do something and then I followed the end of my nose."

Stata Center, Cambridge, USA, 2000–04

Gehry's handling of natural light allows his buildings to become much more than mere sculptural ensembles and to effectively transcend any superficial impression they might seem to give as contrived sculptural ensembles. Especially impressive is Gehry's instinctive sense for choosing just the right kind of light from the fitting solar orientation and directing it into the interior spaces.

His Vitra Design Museum employs skylights oriented in different directions to bathe each exhibition hall in its own individual light. The grand auditorium of the Disney Concert Hall has a generous skylight and a large window front that allows light to illuminate daytime concerts, whereas the lobby spaces receive a combination of natural light from skylights and side windows that makes the white ceiling and wall surfaces seem to glow.

And the architect's use of natural light becomes more refined with each new project. In MIT's Stata Center vertical slits alternate with an array of varied skylights to create a series of differentiated spaces along the building's passage-like "student street." In the recent MARTa Museum in Herford, Germany, Gehry uses skylights to modulate the undulated waves of the exhibition space ceilings and to create a spatial hinge between the existing, remodeled building wings and the new exhibition halls.

Disney Concert Hall, Los Angeles, USA, 1988–2003

Varied natural lighting emphasizes the special nature of each piece on exhibit.

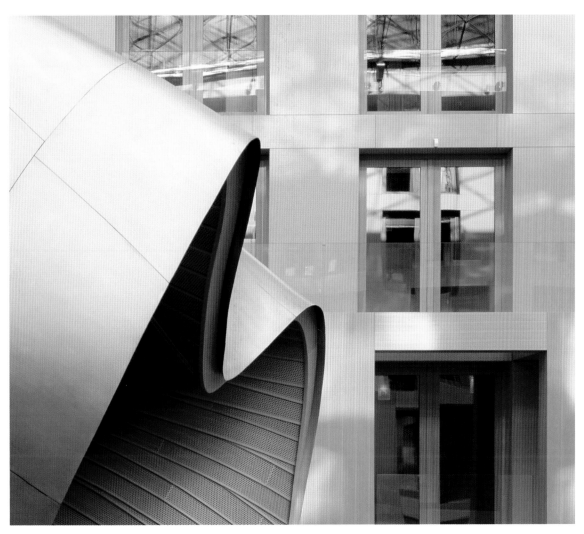

Sculptural forms assume a special presence when they are bathed in carefully directed natural light.

Stata Center, Cambridge, USA, 2000–04

Nationale Nederlanden Building

Prague, Czech Republic
1992–1996

Ginger, Fred and the Wave

Entrusted with the one-time task of designing a mixed-use office building on one of the few sites in Prague's historical city center where new building has been permitted since the fall of the Iron Curtain in 1989, Gehry rose to the occasion.

By breaking up the building volume into distinct yet clearly interrelated elements he achieved an expressively singular composition that sensitively responds to the scale of the surrounding historic structures while delineating the possibilities of freedom of expression offered by the democratic system that has been in place in this former Eastern Bloc country since 1989.

To modulate the building mass and respond to the larger context with the riverfront to the south and a major street to the west Gehry devised three clearly defined building volumes he cheekily deemed "Ginger," "Fred" and "the Wave."

The architect's riverfront facade, termed "the Wave," responds to the larger scale of the river with an undulating surface punctuated by shifting window perforations. The corner is accentuated with a cylindrical tower element, coined "Fred," that is crowned with a dome-like metal sculpture. "Ginger," the tapering glass tower nestled into the side street, culminates the dynamic composition with juxtaposed, transparent verticality.

The 58,000 square foot building houses shops and a café on the ground floor, high-end offices on the upper floors and a rooftop restaurant, which features spectacular views of the Prague skyline and the monumental Hradschin castle across the river.

A vivacious exuberance, reminiscent of the historic Jugendstil architecture found in abundance in Prague, permeates the design. Yet, rather than taking a postmodern approach toward the imposing historical context and copying it with sentimental forms, Gehry succeeds in creating a distinctly new building that strikes up a convincing synthesis with the historical surroundings and effectively transcends them as well.

The expressionist forms effectively reinterpret Kafka's city in an intriguing way that is at once bound in tradition and at the same time looks forward to Prague's new brighter future as one of Middle Europe's most vital capital cities.

Ebene +5

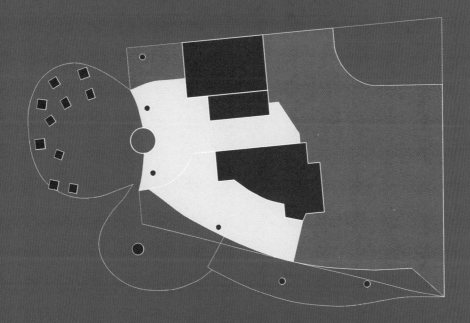

Erdgeschoss

The tapering glass tower, nicknamed Ginger, culminates the dynamic composition with transparent verticality.

A vivacious exuberance, reminiscent of Jugendstil
architecture, permeates the design.

The composition
responds to the scale
of the surrounding
historic structures.

A ribbon window with slanted glazing elements directs natural light into the interior spaces from above.

The generous circulation spaces on the upper floors relate a sense of representation and express the fact that this is more than just a mere functional office building.

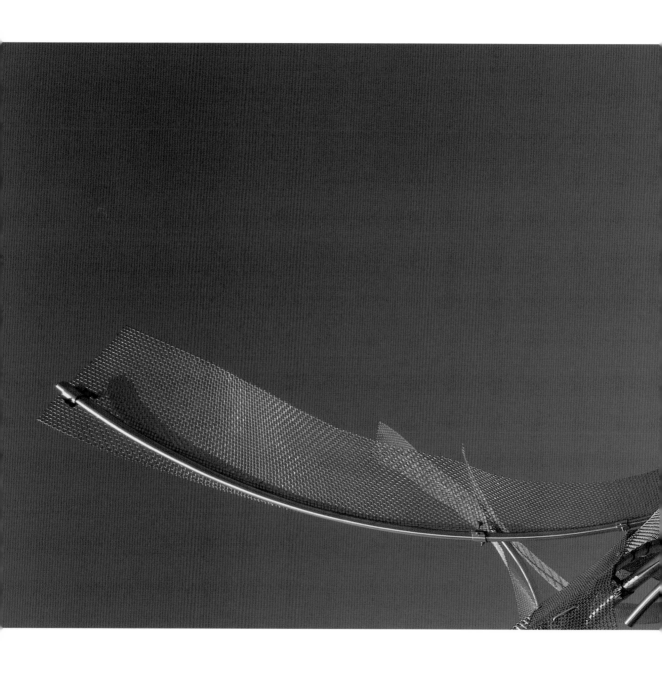

Stainless steel mesh was used to veil the corner tower at the roof terrace level. The restaurant located here offers spectacular views of the Prague skyline.

Der Neue Zollhof

Düsseldorf, Germany
1994–2001

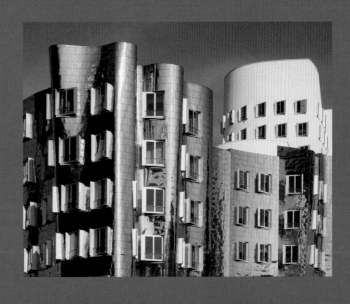

Trinity of Contrasts

Gehry's innovative office complex, located on a former industrial port site in Düsseldorf, Germany, quieted even his most adamant critics. Their argument that his architecture is merely an ecstasy of forms with confetti-like superficiality is countered by this design's spectrum of pragmatic solutions that make these buildings both economically successful and user-friendly.

Taking the extra time necessary to create a unique sculptural composition, Gehry provided both the client and the city of Düsseldorf with a landmark building complex that not only meets the client's needs for attractive commercial and office spaces but also provides the city with an evocative new trademark that has long since ensconced itself in the city's and region's contemporary cultural and architectural consciousness.

To keep the feeling of the project light and airy Gehry envisioned a trinity of three clearly separate building sculptures. Coined "Mother, Father and Child," the ensemble forms a harmonious whole, even though each building has a different facade surfacing of earthy-brown brick, glowing white stucco rendering or shimmering stainless steel.

Compacting the project's 260,000 square feet into mid-rise towers left open spaces free in which the architect created some of the city's most popular urban plazas along Düsseldorf's successful new waterfront promenade. The compact massing also allows expansive views across the cityscape from a surprisingly high number of offices due to the resultant increase in the building periphery and exterior wall surfaces that allow most of the offices to be located on an exterior wall.

The office-level floor plans allow flexible use as either open offices or individual office spaces. The office floors can therefore be rented to separate firms or combined to house larger companies — this resultant flexibility increases desirability and makes it easier to find tenants and accommodate their individual needs.

The construction and design technology used here also blaze new, previously unexplored architectural trails. Integration of innovative drafting and modeling software enabled translation of Gehry's ideas directly into the forms for the prefabricated concrete elements, which could then be produced on the right schedule and within the strict cost limits bindingly set by the investor

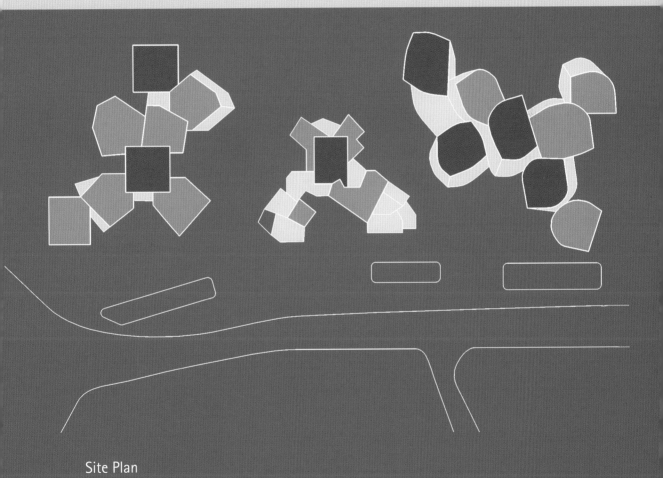

Site Plan

The compact grouping in three building masses allows expansive views across the cityscape for as many offices as possible.

Each building received a
different facade material of
brick, plaster or stainless steel.

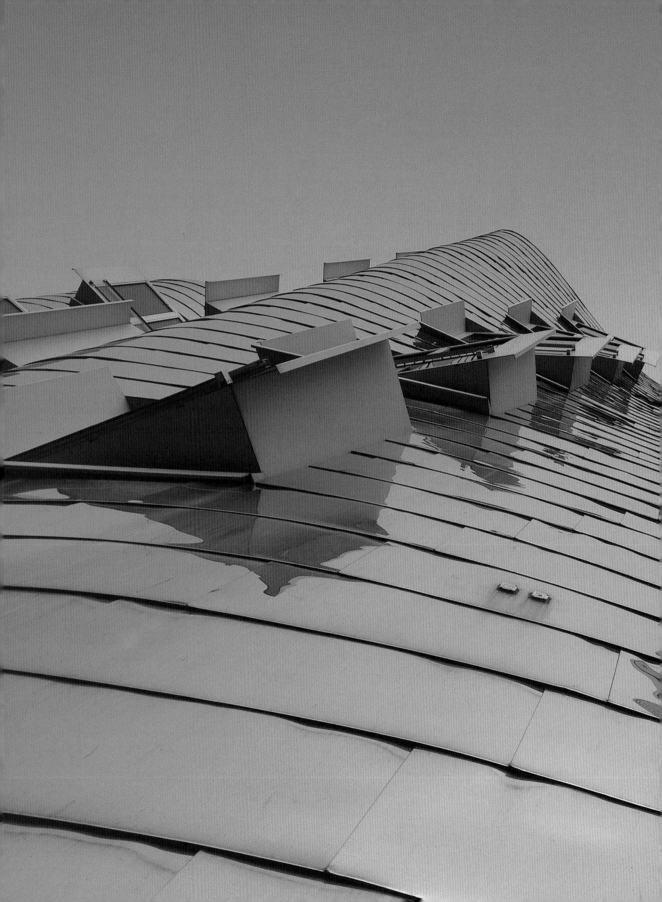

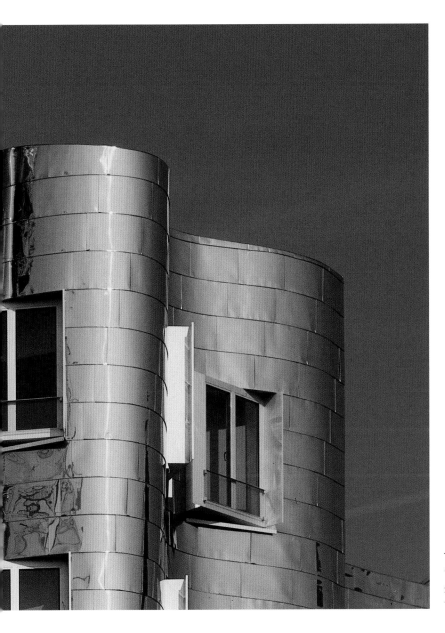

The middle building, coined the "Child," is sheathed in stainless steel and changes appearance throughout the day.

365

Brick, a common material in Düsseldorf, is used on the second highest tower.

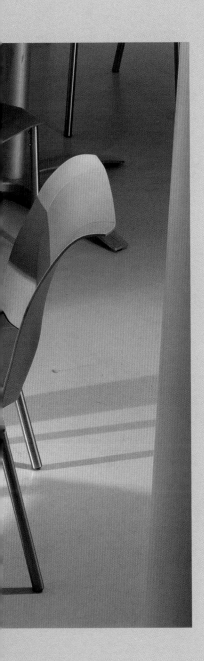

FOG Furniture

Knoll International
1999

Elegance in Metal

When approached by Knoll International to develop yet another line of designer furniture Gehry translated his increased experience in working with metal, the material increasingly prevalent in his architecture since the 1980s, into new furniture forms.

Given the fact that the use of metals in diverse ways has given his most evocative newer works, such as the Guggenheim Museum in Bilbao or the Neuer Zollhof project in Düsseldorf, their nonreplicable, individual expression, it is only fitting that Gehry's FOG series for Knoll International further explores the possibilities and potentials inherent in metal as a material that is excellently suited for conveying his expressive visions in both architecture and design.

The 1999 FOG metal chair is a lightweight, stackable indoor/outdoor piece that was designed in two versions. The basic chair version is an elegant piece without arms, whereas a second model includes elegant metal arm pads made of anodized cast aluminum. Made entirely of metal, the FOG series chairs feature a contoured seat with back and arm pads made of polished, anodized cast aluminum and a frame of tubular stainless steel.

FOG's unique articulated form derives from Gehry's fascination with irregularity and with the calculus of the complex curves that increasingly have distinguished his buildings. Like his recent architecture, it features planes of metal that are strategically creased to define the expressive, elegant forms and lines of Gehry's perhaps lightest and most gracious furniture series.

Observing that his earlier furniture was "designed as a kind of reaction against the usual expectations of the furniture market," Gehry says that the FOG chair is even more genuine and that it "comes out of my own work, the shapes of my buildings." The ribs and creases that articulate the aluminum seat and back provide both structural rigidity and visual interest. The seat and back are separate, and Gehry exploited this segmented design to purposefully differentiate between these two aluminum parts. The chairs stack three high. The back angle attachment flexes five degrees for increased seating comfort.

Simple round tables, with either metal or glass surfaces, complete the elegant FOG line of metal furniture.

The ribs and creases that articulate the aluminum seat and back provide both structural rigidity and visual interest.

"The FOG chair comes out of my own work, from the shapes of my buildings."

Made entirely of metal, it features a contoured seat with back and arm pads made of polished, anodized cast aluminum.

Simple round tables complete the elegant FOG line of metal furniture.

Pariser Platz 3

Berlin, Germany
1994–1999

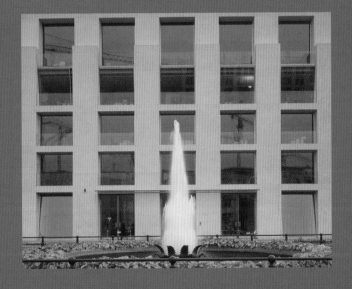

Twisted Grid

Most of the most prominent new projects built in Berlin since the fall of the Berlin Wall in 1989 were built according to the city's then strict design restrictions, which were internationally ridiculed as overly conservative and binding on the architect's creativity.

And on this site, in direct proximity to the Brandenburg Gate, Germany's perhaps most enigmatic national monument, the regulations were especially restrictive. Yet this office building for a German bank that Gehry describes as "one of the best and most radical I have ever built" proves that a creative interpretation of binding planning regulations can generate extraordinary urban design and architectural results.

Taking the materials and proportions bindingly stipulated for the plaza facade as a point of departure, the architect developed an abstract facade grid that at first glance seems to be classicist, as are the surrounding reconstructed buildings around the Pariser Platz square that fronts the Brandenburg Gate. Further study reveals a subtle minimalism that adamantly redefines and defies the tight planning restrictions while simultaneously forming a dignified background for the nearby Brandenburg Gate.

facade, the undulating southern facade that faces on to the adjacent Holocaust Monument, designed by Peter Eisenman, is composed of gentle waves that create bay windows with excellent views of the surrounding cityscape for the apartments within.

The building's interior unites the contrasting design languages used on the northern and southern facades of the exterior. A regular grid of window openings perforates the oak-sheathed walls of the light-bathed interior courtyard. This dignified backdrop highlights the sculptural forms of the central meeting pavilion located in the central court, which enlivens the court like an exotic sea animal surfacing for air from the ocean's deepest depths.

At night, suddenly visible from the plaza, its striking forms contrast the austere plaza front with the building's dynamic inner life. A free-spanning glass roof shelters the central courtyard and forms an urban landmark for the building when seen from a distance or from above, such as when visitors to the nearby Reichstag Parliament building ascend to the top of its glass dome, designed by Norma Foster, and look down on the new Pariser Platz urban ensemble.

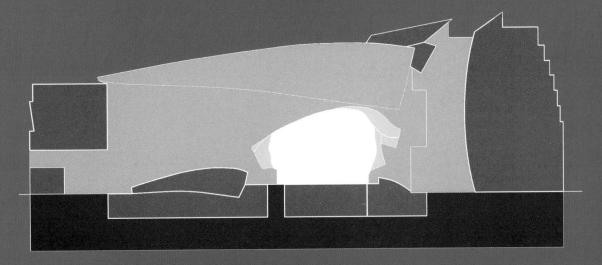

Section

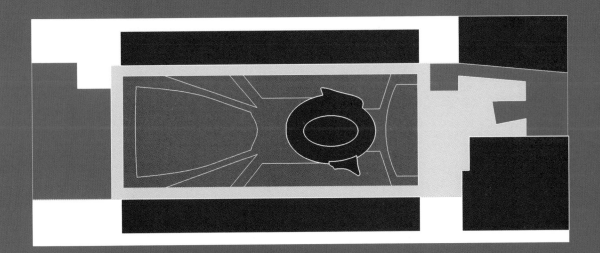

Ground Floor Plan

This building proves that a creative reinterpretation of building regulations can generate extraordinary results.

The southern elevation counters the more strict order of the northern facing
front on Pariser Platz.

The courtyard-facing facades are clad in oak wood paneling. The glass roof
above protects the courtyard from the weather.

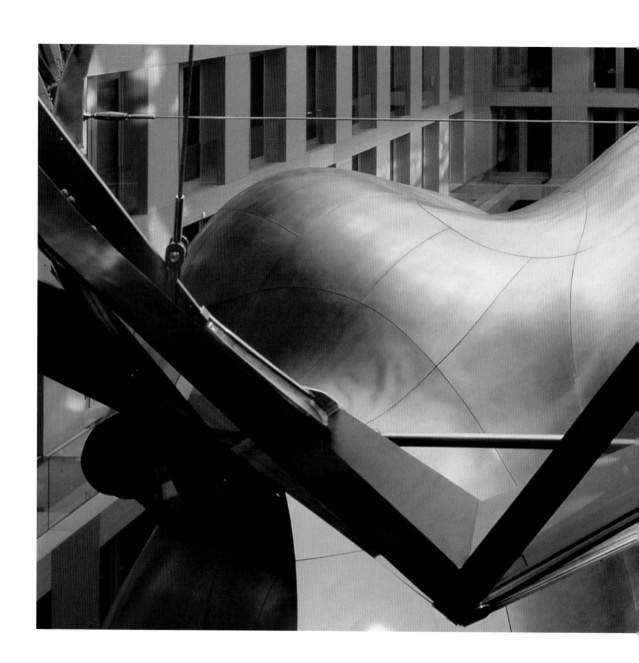

The meeting space in the inner courtyard was completed years after the rest of the building. Several firms were unable to translate the visionary forms into reality.

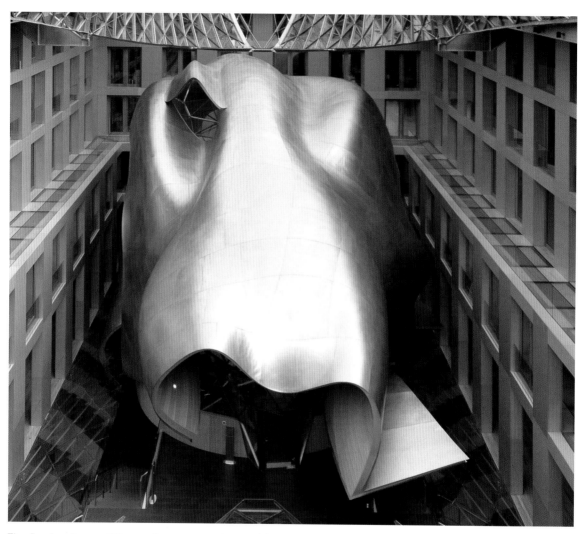

The flowing forms of the conference room inserted into the interior courtyard create a striking contrast to the stricter order of the courtyard facades.

All surfaces inside the conference room were foreseen in wood. The combination of smooth surfaces with perforated panels enhances the acoustic performance of the space.

Special care was taken in the development and implementation of all of the architectural details. The goal was to reach a high level of precision and at the same time create an elegant sense of lightness.

Glass roofs separate the spaces in the ground floor of the courtyard from the
offices above.

The courtyard meets the sky at the seemingly hovering glass roof vault.

Above the rooftops of Berlin on the roof terrace at Pariser Platz.

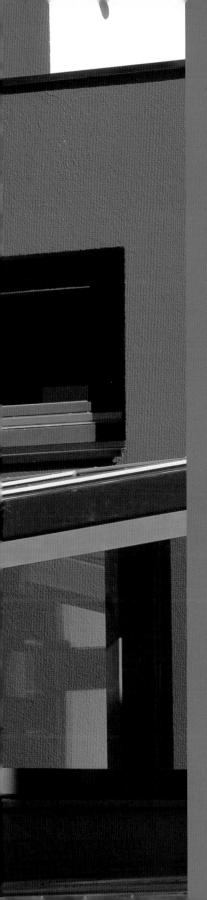

Ronald McDonald
House

Bad Oeynhausen, Germany
1999–2002

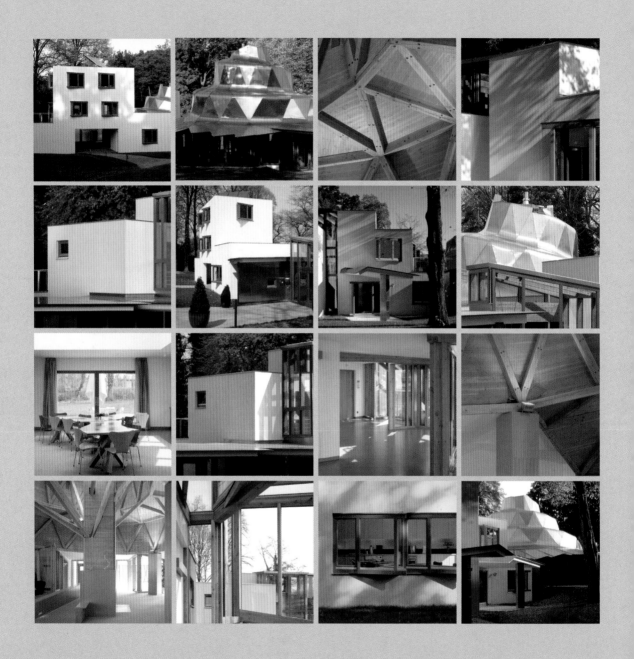

Bringing Light to Darkness

Since 1974, the nonprofit organization Ronald McDonald House Charities has created a worldwide network of special buildings that provide parents and family members of seriously ill children with inexpensive lodging in direct proximity to the hospitals where the children are in treatment for serious illnesses such as cancer or cardiac disease. The resultant increased contact between family members and the young patients often results in especially good treatment results, which have been proven by a convincing reduction in the length of the children's hospital stays by one third.

The Ronald McDonald House in Bad Oeynhausen was initiated by Professor Hans Meyer, a noted doctor practicing at the nearby Clinic for Inborn Cardiac Defects. When Professor Meyer asked Gehry to design the building, the architect didn't hesitate. It was clear from the outset that this was a project he wanted to support, as he has done with social projects many other times throughout his long career.

Gehry set a design team to work on the project with the premise of creating an intimately scaled, village-like complex where both children and their parents could feel at ease and protected while at the same time ensuring a high-quality, modern health care infrastructure and contemporary physical and mental treatment therapies.

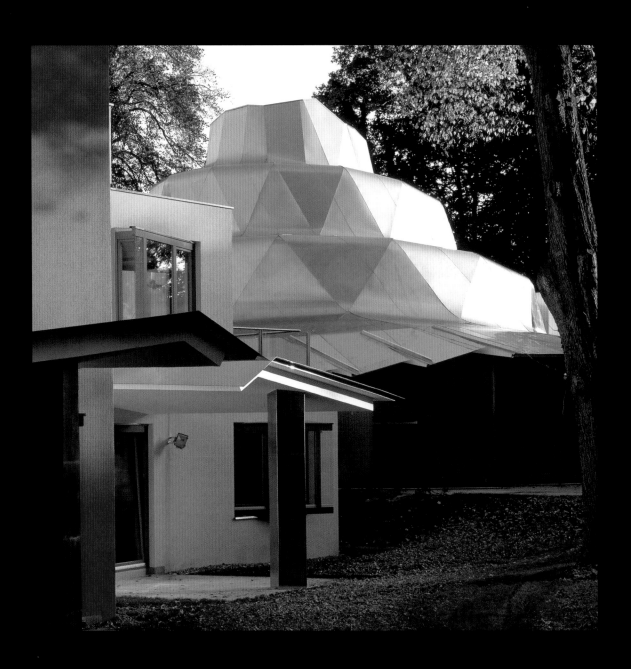

The "Maypole," a round pavilion with a shiny metal roof and an exposed wooden structural skeleton inside, forms the clearly defined heart of the composition and provides the families with both real and symbolic shelter.

The other buildings of the complex form a village of interconnected houses. Their bright colors successfully incorporate just the right scale to make families and young patients feel as much at home as possible. To form a more sensitive background, milder colors were used for the interior spaces, where wood is the prevalent material.

The light-filled building, located in Bad Oeynhausen's Spa Gardens, has been home to over 10,000 people since it opened in 2001.

As such, it tells a real success story made possible through Gehry's especially sensitive and wistful design, which puts people and their needs at the forefront and avoids seemingly forced architectural statements to create a relaxed environment of healing.

The buildings form a village of interconnected, brightly colored houses.

Windows and entrance porches
help define the individual
character of each pavilion.

Milder colors were used for the interior spaces, where wood is
the prevalent material.

Building with Wood

Natural Warmth

One singular phenomenon unites all of Gehry's buildings — all of them invite use and emanate a deeply intrinsic warmth. This central design aspect is one of the major keys to understanding the undeniable success of Gehry's works. One method for achieving this quality lies in the use of warmth-emanating interior materials that effectively contrast with the often cool materials used on the buildings' exteriors. This allows both material worlds — such as stainless steel on the outside and wood paneling on the inside — to assume their fullest possible effect. The contrast between the stark outdoors, including the harshness of the subconsciously perceived "outside world" and the relaxed ease of Gehry's "interior worlds," is precisely designed and foreseen, sometimes based on calculated perception but oftentimes founded in Gehry's gut feeling for creating just the right atmosphere every time.

In his early works Gehry used the material most readily and economically available to him — Douglas fir framing lumber. To let the wood enlighten the spaces and make them seem unfinished and informal Gehry left the framing lumber visible in his 1970s residential projects in and around Los Angeles, such as the Davis Studio and Residence in Malibu (1968–72), the Norton Simon Gallery and Guest House in Malibu (1974–76) and his own home in Santa Monica (1977–78; 1991–94). On his own house he used framing lumber to nail together a moonstruck-collage pergola that all but immortalizes America's perhaps most enigmatic and common building material.

Disney Concert Hall, Los Angeles, USA (1988–2003)

Later works see the increased use of hardwood, planed softwoods and plywood, such as in the oak parquet flooring of the Vitra Design Museum or the hardwood paneling used on the courtyard facades of the Pariser Platz 3 project in Berlin.

The entire interior of the Disney Concert Hall is paneled in warm Douglas fir that greatly enhances the hall's acoustical performance. The Bard Theater also uses hardwoods extensively as paneling on the tiers and as billowing ceiling elements. Another performance structure where wood was deployed to create a warm contrast to the extensive metal exterior surfaces is the recently completed Millennium Park Bandstand in Chicago, where Gehry deployed acoustic wood panels as the backdrop for the orchestra stage.

Gehry also skillfully uses wood to enrich his buildings for charitable organizations, such as the Ronald McDonald House in Bad Oeynhausen, Germany, or Maggie's Cancer Centre in Dundee, Scotland, where it helps define especially sensitive, warmth-emanating places for healing.

Whereas wood often stands in marked contrast to the metal surfaces of the exteriors, it is complemented on the interiors with smooth concrete, stone, smooth white rendering and glass surfaces.

Bard Theater, Annandale, USA (2000–03):
Inside Gehry's buildings wood forms a
warm contrast to the abstract coolness of
the materials used outside.

Millennium Park, Chicago, USA (1999–2004)

Maggie's Cancer Centre (2000–2003):
Exposed framing timber remains one
of Gehry's favorite materials.

MARTA Museum, Herford, Germany (2002–05)

Bard Theater

Annandale, New York
2000–2003

Confetti Landscape

Already touted as the new cultural nucleus of the Hudson Valley, the recently completed Fisher Center in upstate New York draws attention to a scenic region known up until now more for the renown landscape painters of the Hudson River School, who immortalized it with their moving works in the 1800s, than for provocative or progressive architecture such as the engaging complex created here by Frank O. Gehry.

Taking the site's unique natural setting and the region's famous tradition of landscape painting into full account when he set out to design this project, Gehry sensitively conceived the building as an autonomous object set amid the pristine landscape that enhances the campus and contrasts with and augments the surrounding park landscape with its majestic, towering trees. The titanium metal panels Gehry organically wrapped around the building help reduce its optical mass and effectively merge it with the landscape, without emulating or imitating the lush surrounding natural setting in any direct way.

Unfolding up toward the center of the composition, the metal panels open to rise up to a blossom-like virtual center where the building merges with the sky above.

Two theaters, four rehearsal studios for dance, theater,
and music as well as professional support facilities are
all contained within the 110,000 square foot mixed-use
facility on the edge of the Bard College campus.

In spite of the large building mass that includes high
fly towers for the professional concert stages, Gehry
managed to carefully cloak the mass in undulating, light
forms so the complex appears well scaled and in tune
with the surrounding historic campus architecture of
the adjacent historic college setting.

The intimate, 900-seat Sosnoff Theater has an orchestra
space, parterre and two balcony sections. It features an
orchestra pit for opera and an acoustic shell designed
by Yasuhisa Toyota, making it a first-class concert hall
for performances of chamber and symphonic music.
Theater Two was designed to be especially flexible to
accommodate Bard College's varied theater and
dance programs.

During the academic year the facility is used for college
productions. In summer, the center transforms into
a regional public arts facility that hosts established
international workshops and festivals.

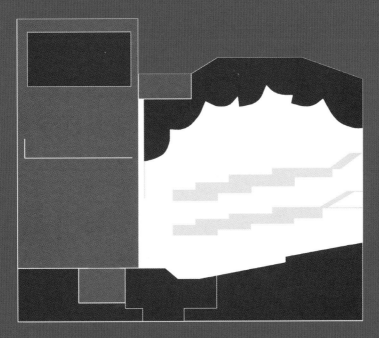

Section

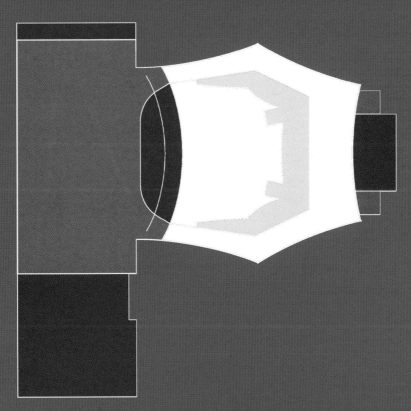

Schematic Ground Floor Plan

The panels wrapping around the building reduce its optical mass and merge it with the landscape, without emulating it.

Low service wings adjoin the fly tower.

The titanium steel facade surfaces rise directly up out of the lawns to additionally heighten the contrast between architecture and nature.

The compact foyer space

The interior sides of the metal roof surfaces and the steel structural framework were exposed in the foyers.

The intimate, 900-seat Sosnoff Theater has an orchestra, parterre and two balcony sections.

Maggie's Cancer Centre

Dundee, Scotland
2000–2003

A Place of Caring

Maggie Keswick Jencks, the wife of noted architectural historian Charles Jencks, fostered the idea of building small cancer care centers across the United Kingdom before her death from breast cancer in 1995. All of the various centers are designed by noted and celebrated architects and are guided by the conviction that buildings can play a major role in supporting cancer patients.

As such, these intimately designed building settings may help sufferers somehow better manage their fears and deal with the insurmountable pressures and anxieties cancer unexpectedly faces them, their families and loved ones with.

Gehry, a close friend of Maggie and Charles Jencks, waved his fee for this project, as he often has for other charitable projects, such as the Ronald McDonald House in Bad Oeynhausen, Germany. This project was financed through charitable donations and local fund-raising and opened its doors in 2003.

The Centre sits on the gentle slope of a hill overlooking the magnificent natural landscape panorama of Scotland's Tay Estuary. To best express and capture the unique setting Gehry built over 70 design models before he finally settled on the essential design with its quintessential elements.

The central tower was inspired by nearby lighthouses, whereas the asymmetrically folded roof was based on a pattern of a shawl worn by a woman in a Vermeer portrait Gehry saw in a museum together with Maggie. These associative design elements imbue the project with meaning and interconnect it to local building tradition and the intimate sense of caring conceived by Maggie Keswick Jencks.

The latticework roof is built of Finnish pine and laminated plywood and finished with stainless steel. In an effort to create a unique place of caring the architect virtually eliminated boring right angles and dull repetitive elements.

The Centre houses a communal therapy room, a kitchen, an information area and a circular library. Intimate niches offer spaces to be alone and contemplate the landscape.

In making sure that each space was carefully dimensioned to serve as a well-scaled place of healing and caring, Gehry didn't waste a square inch of the small building, which contains merely 2,000 square feet of floor space.

The Royal Fine Arts Commission Trust honored the building, Gehry's first in the UK, as "Building of the Year" in 2004.

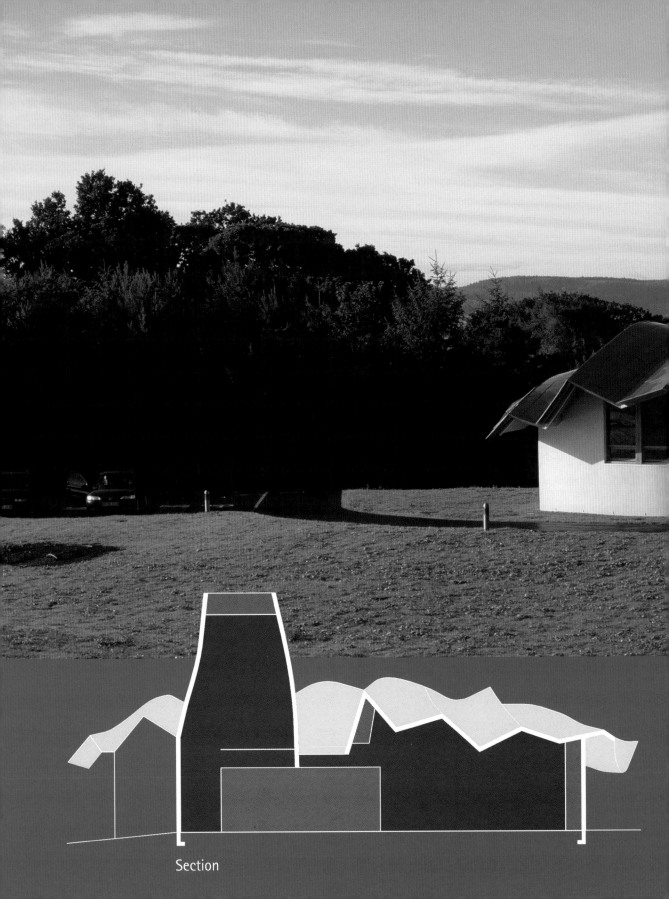

Section

In an effort to create a unique place of caring Gehry virtually eliminated
right angles and repetitive elements.

The roof forms echo the
contours of the landscape.

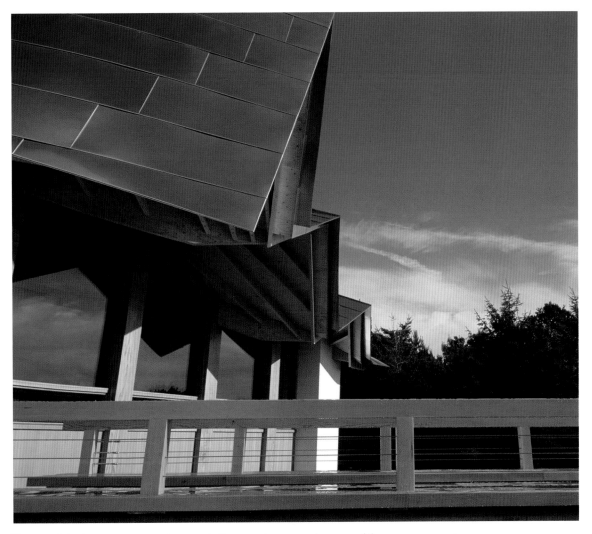

The wood deck serves as an entrance platform and as a sun terrace with
views out to the Scottish landscape.

The wide eaves offer protection from sun and weather and create a gradual transition between architecture and nature.

The central space of the small building is used for the reception area, which directly adjoins the library.

Stata Center

Cambridge, Massachusetts
2000–2004

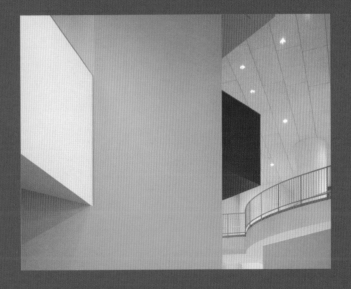

Robots at a Party

Built to accommodate some of the world's most noted scientists, Gehry's design for this university building at the prominent MIT campus in Cambridge, Massachusetts, celebrates the "joy of invention" while inspiring its denizens to even higher achievement.

The building's manifold forms — the architect describes it as looking like "a bunch of drunken robots got together to celebrate" — delineate a vast 730,000 square foot complex containing offices, laboratories, lecture halls, a fitness center, kitchens, a child care center, a below-ground parking garage, an outdoor amphitheater and a café.

A survey of MIT students in 1998 showed that they missed communal spaces for interaction. This inspired Gehry to incorporate a two-lane, double-height "student street" that weaves through the interior of the complex, connecting a number of spacious common areas such as the cafeteria, auditoriums and seminar rooms.

These areas are modulated with bright splashes of red, yellow and blue and receive light from a range of skylights, imbuing each with an individual quality — all in an effort to "lure the orangutans out of their trees" so that students can interrelate in the common areas, allowing synergy and capacitating lively academic discourse.

To give scale to the large, eight- to nine-story high building masses Gehry opted for modulating the building into countless building wings and masses that are clad in various materials.

Brick, a material commonly used throughout the MIT campus, was used to clad several of the towering building wings. These alternate with towers clad in various metal sheeting materials that include stainless steel, galvanized and powder-coated metal sheeting and corrugated metal roofing. The perforated window openings and regular forms of the brick-clad towers were carefully juxtaposed with the more exuberant forms and the protruding window bays of the metal-clad towers.

The building is massed to create a coherent backbone in front of which the pavilion-like structures of the auditorium and cafeteria roofs stand like sculptural objects adeptly placed by Gehry upon the brick plinth that forms the formative solid base of the building and contains the ground-floor spaces.

The verticality of the grand interior communal areas contrasts with the individual office spaces — intimate zones where scientists can retreat and concentrate.

These spaces are just right, according to resident scientist Tim Berners-Lee — credited with inventing the World Wide Web — because the windows can be opened "to let fresh air in."

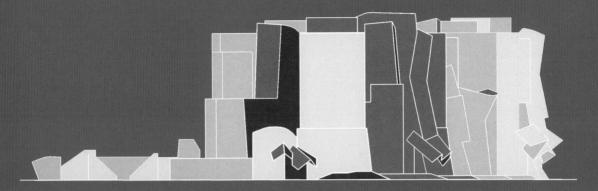

Elevation

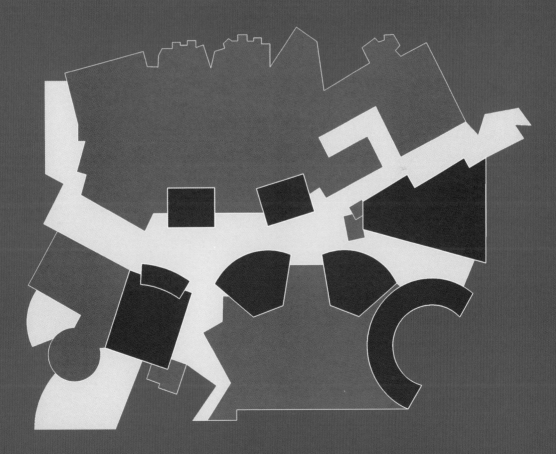

Ground Floor

The building's manifold forms — Gehry describes it as looking like "a bunch of drunken robots got together to celebrate" — contain 730,000 square feet.

The amphitheater continues
the interior "student street"
outdoors.

The building masses are distributed and contained in individual building elements that are clad with various materials in order to avoid repetition and accommodate human scale.

The buildings form a courtyard within which special building elements such as lecture halls are placed. The shiny metal roof surfaces reflect light into the "student street" on the ground floor.

The courtyard is formed by a veritable "family" of diversely sculpted building elements. Special functions, such as the lecture hall sheathed in yellow metal panels, are emphasized as free-standing objects on the plateau.

Scientists' offices all have their own windows, which can be opened.

Although the "student street" crosses the wide depth of the building it is light-filled and pleasant. This is ensured by various skylights and ample large glazing elements that bring light in from above and from the side.

Bright colors mark the focal points along the "student street."

The generous "student street" is Gehry's effort to "lure the orangutans out of their trees" and into the common areas.

32 | Dreyfoos Bldg ↑ | Gates Bldg → |
| Washrooms ← | Main St → |

The cafeteria furniture was also designed by Gehry. The wooden benches were designed specifically for this space, and the chairs are from the FOG series manufactured by Knoll International.

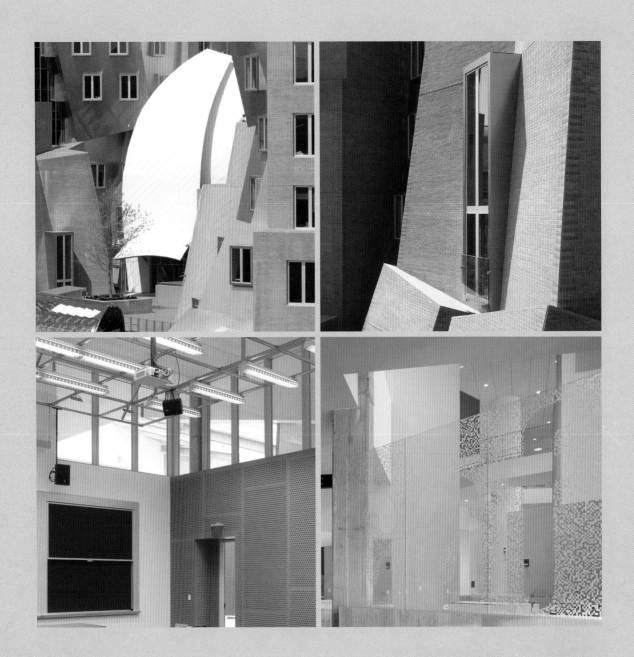

Marta Museum

Herford, Germany
2002–2005

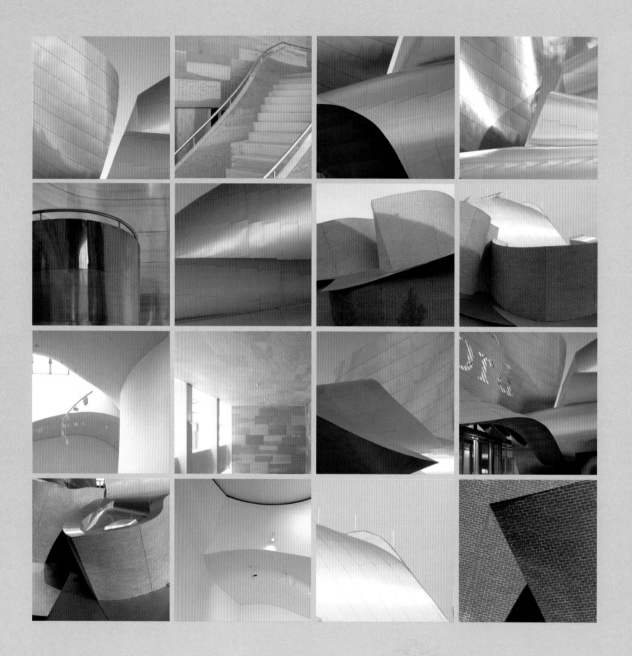

More than a Museum

Contemporary museums demand new concepts. A museum can no more be seen as merely an institution where art is presented in an aesthetic vacuum. A new generation of art lovers who will travel far to visit the latest museums and exhibitions has established itself as a powerful economic factor.

Additionally, due to the reduction of public subsidies, present-day museums must also be conceived and led as commercially viable institutions capable of successfully supporting themselves.

This is also the case in Herford, where even the name of the museum seeks to reflect these necessities: the name MARTa stands for M (Möbel/furniture), ART (art) and a (ambience) and makes it clear that this contemporary institution is much more than just a museum.

Gehry transformed this vision into reality by creating variegated spatial zones that altogether form an ensemble in the midst of the smugness of the small town that playfully provokes and effectively draws attention onto itself. From the central foyer that is accessed from a entry plaza recessed between the building forms visitors move on to either the "Forum for Culture, Events and Presentations," the "Museum for Art and Design" or the "Competency and Information Center" housed in the former factory building built in the 1950s, which Gehry clad in wood on the interior and surfaced in Bauhaus-reminiscent white rendering on the exterior.

The exhibition spaces, foreseen completely in white and solely lit from above by skylights, form a spatial framework that is especially well suited to presenting art and design exhibitions.

The irregularly shaped spaces in the events center invite visitors to take part in a lively exchange of ideas far removed from the rigidity common to congress centers the world over.

The convex and concave sculpted facade surfaces clad in brick reinterpret the use of this regionally typical building material in an unconventional way that invites visitors to come inside and engage with this unique building.

Elegantly sculpted metal roof surfaces wrap down from above to effectively merge ground plane, walls, roofs and the sky and mark the generous entrance to the foyer, which serves as a distribution space for the various building functions that are located in refurbished former factory buildings and the new Gehry wings with their expressive, evocative forms.

The warm hues of the brickwork used extend inside into the foyers and restaurant, where various wood and copper surfaces underscore the architect's intention of creating an inviting ambience conducive to cultural activities and communication.

The new ensemble respects the scale of the surrounding buildings yet at the same time creates a striking contrast to the small-town context.

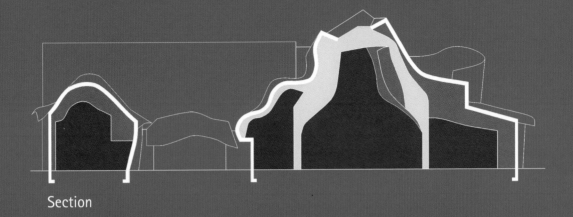

Section

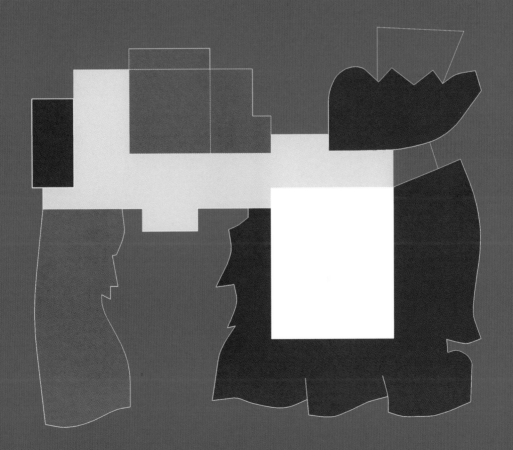

Ground Floor

The entrance forecourt is contained on two sides by new building wings. It leads to the glazed main entrance located at the juncture between new and old building parts.

The waterfront elevation was designed to accommodate the restaurant with its café terrace. The existing, historically listed 1950s factory buildings were fully refurbished and integrated into the new ensemble.

The linearity of the circulation spine that runs parallel to the refurbished factory buildings is played against the flowing spatial composition of the exhibition spaces.

Interior spaces that were "carved" out of the historic factory buildings are sheathed in plywood panels.

The conference rooms paneled in wood and the café sheathed in copper augment the functional and visual concept of the museum complex.

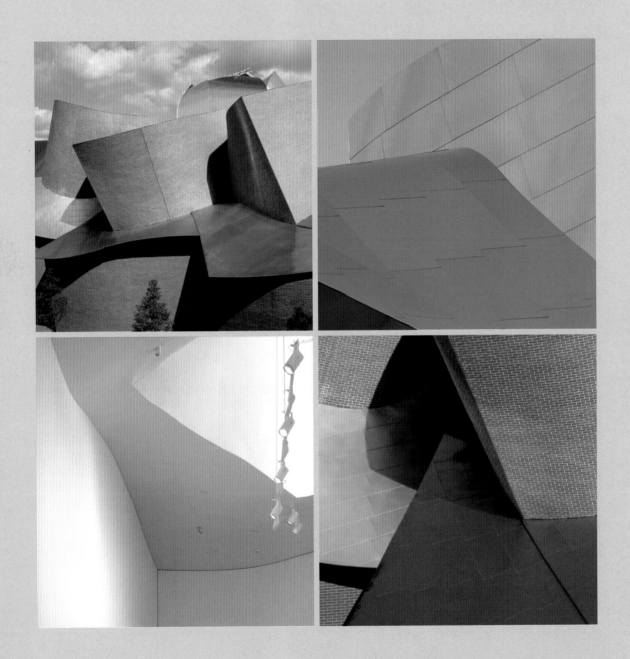

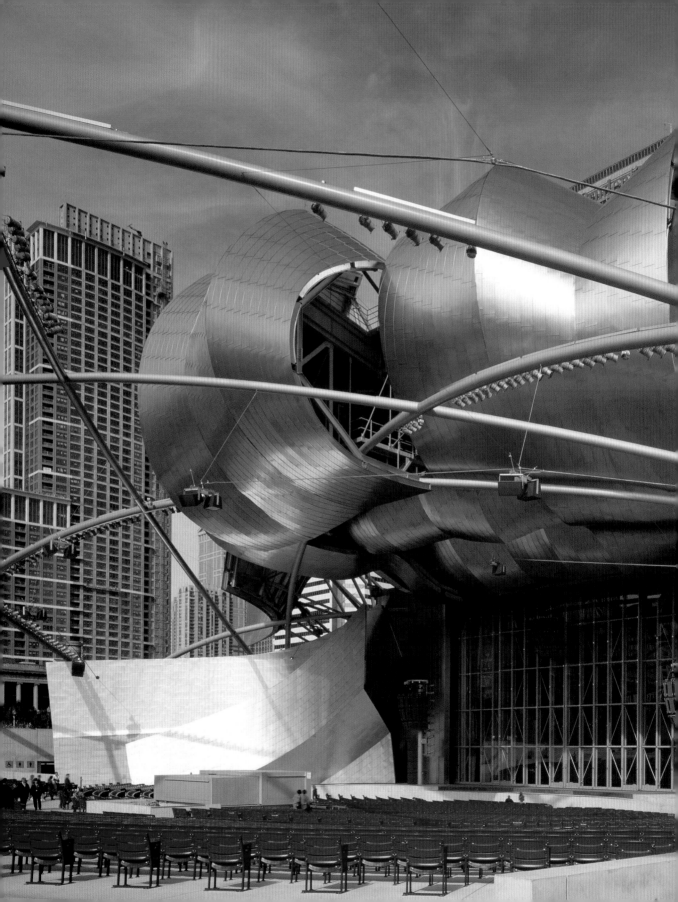

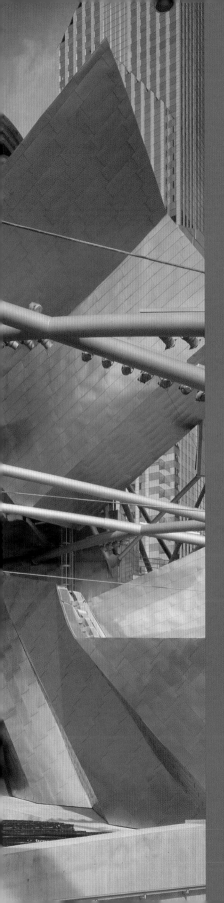

Millennium Park

Chicago, Illinois
1998–2004

Baroque Bandstand

Chicago, the most powerful metropolis of the American Middle West, was one of the eminent birthplaces of the modern movement. It was here that Louis Sullivan declared that "form follows function," a notion that became the guiding concept of modern architecture. And when Mies van der Rohe emigrated here in 1933, the city became home to perhaps the most influential advocate of modernism, whose paradigm "less is more" was based on the theoretical foundations laid by Sullivan.

But the architectural demise of late modernism in Chicago in the late 1970s was accompanied by massive social and building decay in large sections of the inner city. This was a result of the overdimensioned traffic network and functional separations propagated by modern urban planning that led to the dreary mechanization of the city.

This desperate situation was exemplified in multiple locations throughout the city but was perhaps most blatantly evident in the scarring chasm that separated the historic city center from Lake Michigan, where a multilane highway made it difficult for pedestrians in the city center to access Grant Park on the shore of nearby Lake Michigan.

The controversial Millennium Park project, with its landmark buildings by Frank O. Gehry, unfortunately may not have been completed on time for the millennium celebrations in 2000 but has nonetheless become a vibrant new urban node in Chicago's refurbished urban fabric.

The beginning of the new millennium in 2000 marked a turning point for Chicago. Here in Grant Park the city made a bold new start in both urban design and architecture. The new Millennium Park, a public park with Frank O. Gehry's Jay Pritzker Pavilion as its focal building and the elegant, stainless steel–clad BP Bridge that spans an inner-city highway to connect the park to the nearby larger Grant Park on the shore of Lake Michigan, was created as an "urban repair" measure directly adjacent to the vibrant city center with its legendary skyscrapers.

The Jay Pritzker Pavilion, an open-air theater for diverse cultural events, forms the focus of the new Millennium Park complex. Gehry designed a bipartite spectator zone here: red seats invite one to enjoy concerts directly in front of the stage, and a large lawn space offers comfortable seating space for more spectators.

The entire zone is spatially defined by an open framework vault structure made of free-spanning stainless steel pipe sections. The second structure designed by Gehry here, the BP Bridge, snakes elegantly up in stainless steel curves to span across a highly trafficked expressway and create a pedestrian-friendly connection to the shore of nearby Lake Michigan.

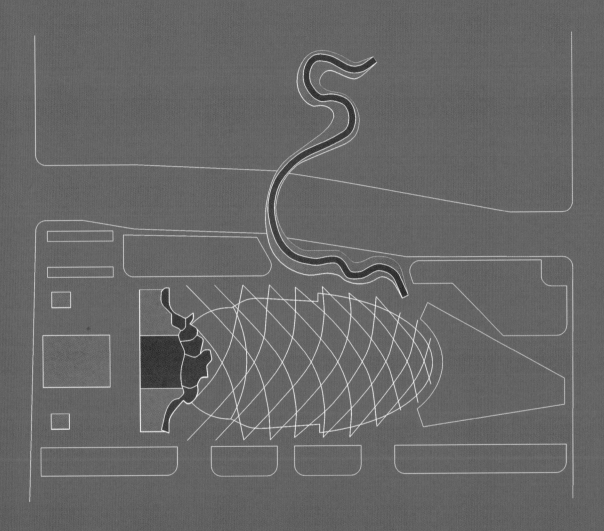

Site Plan

The former neglected site located directly adjacent to a busy expressway was transformed into an attractive urban park.

The moving forms of the Pritzker Pavilion provocatively counter the traditional architectural forms found in downtown Chicago.

Y PRITZKER PAVILION

The spirit of technical innovation long nurtured in Chicago lives on in the exuberant forms and structural precision of the new buildings.

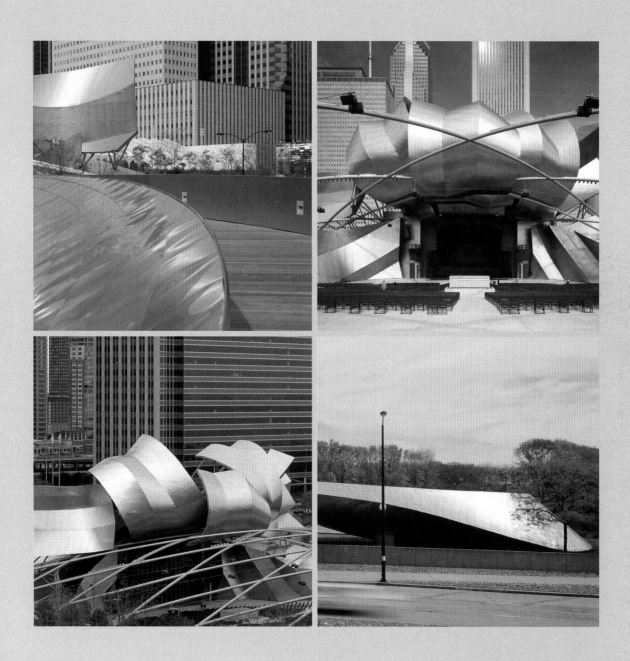

Biography (selected data)

Vital Dates

1929	born Frank Owen Goldberg in Toronto, Ontario, Canada
1947	moved to Los Angeles, California
1954	Name changed from Frank Owen Goldberg to Frank O. Gehry

Architecture Studies

1949–54	College of Architecture, University of California, Los Angeles, California
1956–57	Graduate School of Design, Harvard University, Cambridge, Massachusetts
1979	Spiller Residence, Venice, California

Work Experience 1953–1962

1953–55/57–61	Victor Gruen Associates, Los Angeles, California
1955–56	US Army, Special Service Division, Atlanta, Georgia Robert and Company, Atlanta, Georgia
1957	Perry, Shaw, Hepburn and Dean, Boston, Massachusetts Hideo Sasaki, Boston, Massachusetts
1961–62	André Rémondet, Architecte, Paris, France

Professional Experience 1962–Present

1962–65	Gehry and Walsh, Architects, Santa Monica, California
1966–67	Gehry, Walsh and O'Malley, Baltimore, Maryland
1967–	Frank O. Gehry and Associates, Santa Monica, California, Principal

Selected Completed Projects (by date of completion)

1959	Steeves Residence, Brentwood, California
1964	Projects for Kay Jewelers, Los Angeles, California
1964	Faith Plating Company, Hollywood, California
1965	Danziger Studio and Residence, Hollywood, California
1966	Art Treasures of Japan Exhibition, Los Angeles, California
1967	Merriweather-Post Pavilion, Columbia, Maryland
1968	Public Safety Building, Columbia, Maryland
1972	Davis Studio and Residence, Malibu, California
1973	Easy Edges Furniture
1976	Concord Performing Arts Center, Concord, California
1978	Gehry Residence Phase I, Santa Monica, California
1979	Gemini G.E.L., Los Angeles, California
1979	Cabrillo Marine Museum, San Pedro, California
1979	Spiller Residence, Venice, California
1980	Santa Monica Place, Shopping Center, Santa Monica, California
1981	Indiana Avenue Houses, Venice, California
1982	Experimental Edges Furniture, Thousand Oaks, California
1982	Hollywood Bowl Renovation, Hollywood, California
1983	The Temporary Contemporary Museum, Los Angeles, California
1984	World Expo Amphitheater, New Orleans, Louisiana
1984	California Aerospace Museum, Los Angeles, California
1984	Norton Residence, Venice, California
1985	Rebecca's Restaurant, Venice, California
1986	Goldwyn Library, Hollywood, California

Selected Completed Projects (by date of completion)

1987	Winton Guest House, Wayzata, Minnesota	1992	Bentwood Furniture for Knoll International
1987	Fishdance Restaurant, Kobe, Japan	1992	Vila Olimpica, Barcelona, Spain
1988	University Buildings, UC Irvine, Irvine, California	1993	Weisman Art Museum, Minneapolis, Minnesota
1988	360 Newbury Street, Boston, Massachusetts	1994	Gehry Residence Phase II, Santa Monica, California
1988	Sirmai-Peterson Residence, Los Angeles, California	1994	American Center, Paris, France
1988	Edgemar Project, Santa Monica, California	1996	Goldstein Housing Project, Frankfurt, Germany
1989	Schnabel Residence, Brentwood, California	1996	Nationale-Nederlanden Building, Prague, Czech Republic
1989	Yale Psychiatric Institute, New Haven, Connecticut	1997	Guggenheim Museum, Bilbao, Spain
1989	Vitra Design Museum, Weil am Rhein, Germany	1998	Loyola Law School, Los Angeles, California
1989	Center for the Visual Arts, Toledo, Ohio	1999	FOG Furniture for Knoll
1991	Chiat/Day Building, Venice, California	1999	Pariser Platz 3, Berlin, Germany
1992	Iowa Laser Laboratory, Iowa City, Iowa	2000	USTRA Office Building, Hannover, Germany

Professor, Instructor, Critic

2001	Der Neue Zollhoff, Düsseldorf, Germany
2002	Experience Music Project, Seattle, Washington
2002	Ronald McDonald Haus, Bad Oeynhausen, Germany
2003	Bard Theater, Annandale, New York
2003	Maggie's Cancer Centre, Dundee, Scotland
2003	Walt Disney Concert Hall, Los Angeles, California
2004	Stata Center, Cambridge, Massachusetts
2004	Millennium Park Buildings, Chicago, Illinois
2005	MARTa Museum, Herford, Germany

1971–72	College of Architecture, University of Southern California, Los Angeles, California
1975	Southern California Institute of Architecture, Santa Monica, California
1976	Rice University, Houston, Texas
1977–79, 1988–89, 1998	University of California, Los Angeles, California
1978	Cooper Union, New York, New York
1978	University of Texas, Houston
1979, 1982, 1985, 1987–89	Yale University, New Haven, Connecticut
1980, 1983–84	Harvard University, Cambridge, Massachusetts
1992	Bartlett School of Planning and Urban Design
1996	Federal Institute of Technology (ETH), Zurich, Switzerland
1997	MIT, Cambridge, Massachusetts

Photographers

artur VIEW

architekturbilder agentur gmbh